Nurturing the Mystic Within

A Spiritual Pathway to Lifting the Veil of Fear Blocking the Perception of Paradise

Catherine S. Tuggle

Wood Thrush Publishing
2025

Author photo © Peter Mutschler, PGM Image
pjmimage.mypixieset.com

Book and cover design by Robin Wrighton

ISBN: 979-8-218-48837-6
Library of Congress Control Number: 2025918142

Tuggle, Catherine S.
Nurturing the Mystic Within: A Spiritual Pathway to
Lifting the Veil of Fear Blocking the Perception of Paradise

Wood Thrush Publishing
wendykycatherine@gmail.com

First edition

Printed in the United States of America

To my little kumquat and her two brothers,
who never minced words about my writing.

❧

Contents

Part V: The Pathway Back to Paradise

Man must be sharpened

On man

Like knife on stone.

~ Ancient Chinese Proverb[1]

Preface

On an ordinary autumn afternoon, I clearly heard five words voiced during the most spectacular dream of my life. Understanding the message those words implied was years in the making.

At the time, my husband Ken and I lived in a house surrounded by two acres of white oaks, most welcome for three-quarters of a year until fall. We had just spent a day and a half raking massive tarp-loads of leaves, acorns, and branches and hauling them to a pile behind our garage: a potential fortune of compost. On the second day, after breaking for lunch, both of us had to concede we had pushed our bodies beyond their ability to endure hauling another load. Leaving Ken sprawled out on the library floor, I managed to hoist my aching body up the stairs to our bedroom. Step by wretched step, I finally made it to our bed, flopped down, and immediately fell into a deep sleep. Instantly, the dream began. From its onset, absent was the shadowy quality of most dreams. I was a participant in this dream and aware of everything going on, not an observer as usual.

As the dream ensued, it felt as if I were traveling off somewhere to my right. Then, the movement stopped. While warmth embraced me, I felt immersed in a diffused light, reminiscent of the glow that flows through my fingers when backlighted by a flashlight while steeped in unconditional love. At this point, a voice clearly stated, "All that exists is love." Then, the light began to fade and I realized I was returning to where I had been when the dream started. Upon return, I wondered if I could will myself back to the light. To my surprise, I found I could and did. Plunged for the second time into what can only be described as a sauna of unconditional love, the voice spoke again. This time, it said, "Love is all that exists."

Awe shattered me into full consciousness. The next thing I knew, I was running down the stairs to tell Ken about this astounding dream. As I began crouching down to where he lay on the floor, an inexplicable, even inconceivable, realization dawned on me. My body, which just minutes earlier felt as if it had been the victim of a ten-car pileup, was now *pain-free.* Barely a trace of pain from the grueling labor my body had endured over the last day and a half lingered—*anywhere.* But there in front of me lay Ken, still mired in misery.

Something about the dream actually healed my body!

As I related the experience to Ken, the absurdity of the message struck me dumb. Worst of all, as much as I wanted to write those five words off as one of those perplexing aspects typical of most dreams, I couldn't. The indisputable fact that my body had been healed made ignoring the message out of the question.

Everything about the incident threw my sense of reality into chaos. From the assault on my belief system to the miraculous healing, the experience was fraught with irony. Especially troubling was the idea that the Universe, or God, found me worthy of such a glorious gift. Based on my past, I suspected that if our legal system sent people to jail based on thought alone, for sure I'd be a "lifer," so I had to ask myself, was receiving such a powerful, healing a failure of God's understanding or mine?

The idea that God would confer such a dream upon *me,* of all people, didn't make a bit of sense. Maybe God didn't know the extent of my sins. This made me wonder if *what I'd been taught about God might bear little resemblance about the actuality of God's perception of us.* As bewildering as those five words were—that all that exists is love, words I could ignore—but an instantaneous healing? Turning my back on something as lacking in subtlety as that proved impossible. If the intent was to spark my curiosity about the nature of reality, I have to admit it was an extremely clever strategy. For sure, it made the dream's message impossible to ignore.

Without the healing, the last thing I would have attempted to do was make sense of those five words. I would have chosen do anything instead—iron men's shirts, paint woodwork, dig ditches—rather than try deciphering my dream's message. Since it had been given to me, though, I felt it was mine to fathom. Love is all that exists. Whew! It put everything I thought I knew about reality and God in question. Just listening to the news about the latest war summed up my reality, which couldn't have been more at odds with this message. Considering my lack of expertise, I may as well have been asked to create stock market algorithms than unravel the dream's message.

Aspects of Christianity, psychology, and spirituality clarified certain elements, but none alone could account for all the questions the message raised. Fortunately, lacking a degree in any of these disciplines (and therefore any requisite to remain loyal to them) I had the freedom to draw upon each according to how it clarified the message. At the time I had no idea my journey exploring my dream's message and its implications would transform me in countless ways and inspire me to write this book!

Introduction

I fell in love with my newborn son the moment I set eyes on him; my heart couldn't get enough of Jack. Compared to how my mother loved me there could not have been a bigger contrast. At best, Mother's attitude towards me was indifference. As I grew older, inexplicably her attitude morphed into anger. Years before I had the dream, this enigma had sent me on a quest to understand love: why loving others comes so easily for some people, but for other people it is close to impossible.

After reading numerous books with less than satisfying results, I engaged in a three-year, intensive course on Jungian psychology (this was before the work of Carl G. Jung was deemed acceptable to be taught in universities). Soon after, I picked up a Bible and reread Genesis, chapter 3, about Adam and Eve's time in the Garden of Eden.[2] Applying what I had learned in my Jungian studies to this chapter, the first clue to what inhibited love emerged: fear. Based on this clue, I developed a workshop on a psychological way to grow spiritually.

Considering my metaphorical use of Adam and Eve's plight, I targeted churches as my audience. Every time I prepared to give another workshop, multiple new ideas emerged. It soon became apparent a one-hour presentation was unsuitable. These new concepts were too important to be left out. A book seemed to be the only sensible way to relate these thoughts. That was over thirty years ago.

The first three chapters of Genesis play a prominent role in the spiritual pathway I am proposing. Knowing every culture, such as American Indian tribes, have a different creation story, I suspect the version in the book of Genesis was only one of many renditions that existed when it was picked as our creation story. Without knowledge of the others to mitigate the effect of this version, the traditional interpretation of it has been the sole foundation for human behavior and the characterization of God in cultures that rely on the Bible. For this reason, the first three chapters of Genesis make them the perfect place to begin an in-depth examination of the source of human behaviors that seemingly cannot avoid to produce suffering.

My psychological interpretation of these chapters together with personal experiences form the foundation for my understanding of humanity and our relationship with spirit. For the sake of argument, the basis for the method of spiritual growth I am proposing is the inferred psychological consequences of Adam and Eve's replies to God in the third chapter of Genesis.

The focus of this method is beliefs—in particular how fear functions through our beliefs to affect our potential to connect with spirit and the ability to perceive Paradise. A psychological interpretation of Adam and Eve's answers to God's question in Genesis 3:10, [my wording] "Did you do it, as in eat the apple?" relies on blame. This is dispositive evidence that the first mention of fear in Genesis 3:10, under pressure, morphed. Originating as a mere awareness, their use of blame reveals that fear has changed. It is now functioning unconsciously. As an unconscious influence, fear affects their every perception. The effect of which determines everything

Adam and Eve see and believe—as well as *every human being* thereafter. Even though Biblical verses were inspired by God, one human scribe or another had to document them; therefore, logically, fear unconsciously affected their perceptions too. According to the scribe who wrote Genesis 3:23, God sends Adam and Eve out of the Garden of Eden; however, that is only what that person believed happened. Adam and Eve never left Paradise. Our exquisite blue-green planet is Paradise.

Completing the exercises in Chapter 11 lifts the veil of unconscious fear. With this, the reader comes full circle, back to Adam and Eve's original perception of Paradise. Only one problem. Beliefs stand in the way. For this reason, I offer a brief autobiography to show how fear unconsciously seeded the beliefs that ruled my life.

Due to the fact beliefs come into existence to protect us as children, identifying a problematic belief for the purpose of completing the exercises is close to impossible—after all, that belief originated to protect you as a child even though you are old enough now to protect yourself. The trick is to learn the various expressions of fear well enough to be able to pick up on how they are affecting you. Referring to my autobiographical sketch, I illustrate the various ways I've learned how fear unconsciously disguises beliefs.

Even though this explanation began as way to give readers a way to grow spiritually, my surprise, in the end it unlocked the dream's message. While I do not claim my theory to be irrefutable, two things I purport are true: love is all that exists, and fear impedes our ability to love unconditionally.

The exercises in this book address the unconscious fears that generate conflicts. By engaging in the process of identifying and addressing the unconscious aspect of a fear fomenting a conflict you can eliminate its influence. Eliminating the unconscious effect of a fear erases the veil that has blinded you to the perception of Paradise. You now realize all that exists is love. It becomes your guiding force. A better life for yourself and the world around you results.

PART I

Setting the Stage

Chapter 1

A Terrier on a Tear

The creators of the Second Vatican Council[3] had no clue about how their decree that eating meat on Friday was no longer a sin would affect followers. Had this not happened, I might have turned out like everyone else: wandering through life, trying to figure out how to make money, and then worrying about how to spend it. But that was not to be. I became a terrier on a tear the morning I heard the report of the Vatican's decision. It prompted me to recall the horror stories I'd listened to my mother recount about my grandfather's strict adherence to this particular rule about sin. Now they were saying eating meat on Fridays is no longer an affront to God? How could this be? Even as a twelve-year-old, the cruel joke beliefs make of life struck me hard.

Early on, whenever I found my mother chatting on the phone with one of her sisters, regardless of the opening chatter, I knew the conversation would lead to storytelling before the call ended. Invariably, one of the sisters would bring up one of the many outrageous incidents their father's behavior created. With great anticipation, I waited for the story to begin, burrowing into the chair closest to Mother. Often, the subject was the suffering their father's staunch avoidance of the sin of eating meat on Friday inflicted upon the family.

Granddaddy used the fact that *he* never ate meat on Friday as proof of what a *good* Catholic he was. According to family lore, when my grandmother Babo's finances fell short, the first item she erased from her grocery list was fish for Friday dinner. On these occasions, initially, Babo made bean soup for dinner. Babo used navy beans for her soup, which release quarter-shaped pinkish nuggets into the broth when cooked for a long time. In Granddaddy's mind, the pink nuggets didn't just look like pieces of ham; they *were* ham, even though Babo reassured him they weren't. Even I thought these specks looked like ham. No amount of explanation ever convinced him differently.

Totally invested in the immutability of this mandate and conveniently ignoring that love is paramount to all things Christian, Granddaddy performed a grotesque charade on the Friday nights Babo served him bean soup for dinner. Convinced of his righteousness, he accused his wife of intentionally trying to destroy his standing as a good Catholic. Only when the corpuscles in his face had turned purple, and his wife and children were cowering in the corner of the dining room in tears did he feel confident that he had verified the fact he was a good and righteous Catholic. The trauma her husband's histrionics inflicted on her family became more than Babo could bear. Thereafter, she made bean soup only when Granddaddy was not expected home for dinner on a Friday night.

Regrettably, Granddaddy had been dead for several years when Vatican II revised its stance regarding eating meat on Friday. From then on, Vatican II's decision and the questions it unleashed about *the authenticity of all beliefs* were never far from my thoughts.

The Gift of Insight

The idea that the Church could claim something was a sin one day and then airily dismiss it the next stunned me to the core. This casual dismissal of a sin that the Church had warned against for centuries bothered me—especially in light of how the belief had affected Granddaddy and his family.

When Mother and Daddy married, they decided to leave their churches of origin and joined the Episcopal Church. Even raised as an Episcopalian, I thought sin was a black-and-white matter—period. Hearing that the "powers that be" could suddenly decide a sin was no longer a sin floored me. How could this happen? From then on, I began questioning all beliefs.

Vatican II's decree unwittingly oriented the direction of my life. Its decisions made me wonder what other beliefs are that transitory, that ephemeral. When life presented me with the incident described in the next chapter, I discovered all are.

Thoughts to Ponder

♦ How would it feel to know that something you had believed all your life to be a sin was no longer a sin?

♦ How might the idea that all beliefs are transitory change your attitude? About who or what?

Chapter 2

The Key Incident

This book's premise emerged as I resolved the following incident, which I call my Pivotal Event. Deciphering the elements that gave rise to this event eventually untangled the conundrum posed by the dream's message. Without the jolt of insight from this incident, disentangling the dream's message might never have been possible. Consequently, my beliefs about reality turned inside out.

The sequence of events that occurred during this event established the foundation of my hypothesis about the way fear and beliefs forestall spiritual growth.

The Pivotal Event

The day the Pivotal Event happened it did not strike me as particularly consequential. Unraveling it, however, provided the psychological key to unlocking the dream's message. The insight this incident provided became the foundation for the process of spiritual growth set out in this book.

Like most once-upon-a-time stories, this one began long ago when I was a child. Like most children, to please my parents, unconsciously I guaranteed my place at the family table by absorbing and then parroting their beliefs. Often, the topic of Mother and Daddy's conversations involved the latest shenanigans committed by three of my father's four sisters. The subject of their troublemaking always involved *the factory.*

Sometime in the 1920s, my grandfather decided to start a company that made kitchen cabinets as pieces of furniture that could be moved. Being more of an entrepreneur than someone with sophisticated knowledge, he recognized he needed his son's expertise to achieve his dream. After graduating from Purdue University with a BS in mechanical engineering Daddy had just graduated from the University of Louisville with a degree in law and was in the process of launching a career in politics when his father approached Daddy to help him initiate his latest venture. Turning his back on politics to help his father was not what Daddy wanted. He relented when Grandfather promised him he could leave the company once it got off the ground; however, when that day came, Grandfather panicked. Fearing the company would run aground without my father's expertise, to ensure Daddy's continued presence, Grandfather told him that if he stayed, he would sell Daddy 52% of the company and make him its president. Years earlier, Daddy had purchased several apartment buildings. By selling them, he was able to buy 52% of the factory stock. And so, *with a gentlemen's agreement,* he stayed on as owner and president of the kitchen cabinet business.

Regrettably, on Grandfather's deathbed, perhaps as a way to save face, he told his oldest daughter that he never sold the company to her brother (my father). She, of course, related this "confession" to her sisters. The inconsistencies this admission posed were never questioned. Even after Daddy took over as owner and president of the company, his father never so much as hinted that their arrangement had changed. All but one daughter, Ellen, swallowed her father's version of events. Once planted, the seed of doubt metastasized, setting the stage for family strife, wisps of which still linger even though the company went under years ago. Ah, yes— nothing like deathbed confessions to rev up family lore.

His daughters inherited portions of the company's common stock upon their father's death. Nevertheless, his deathbed statement armed the more gullible of his daughters with a supersized sense of distrust of their brother, ultimately corrupting their attitudes towards Daddy. They contested every decision he made. Not limiting their defiance to contaminating stockholder meetings, they used their inflated sense of righteousness to justify calling my father at all hours of the morning and night. Understandably, Mother disdained these women. Their rancorous pecking was as resolute as turkey vultures over roadkill on a country road. Over the years, during dinner table conversations, Mother must have called her sisters-in-law "greedy" hundreds of times.

By adopting my mother's belief about my aunts' greed, I never questioned my own greedy nature. If they were greedy, I/we were not. We were Ivory-soap-pure. To my way of thinking, my purity was a fact—that is, until Ellen, the only sister who refused to believe the revelation her father made on his deathbed, died when I was in my mid-forties.

Because Ellen never married, my cousins and I were willed to be equal recipients of her largess. At the appointed time for the reading of her will, I found the prospect of joining *them,* the three greedy sisters and their progeny, for the occasion repugnant beyond imagination. After all, *I* was not like *them.* I belonged to the Ivory-soap-pure side of the family. How could someone such as I associate with deplorables such as them? The image I had of my cousins salivating over their prospective booty was just too disgusting for me to have to witness—or so I told myself. Obviously, I shouldn't go. After giving a flimsy excuse, I stayed home and used the time to get an early start on weeding my perennial beds.

Like an overtired, impatient child, resistance to attending the meeting kept gnawing at me, aggravating my thoughts. As I weeded, it suddenly struck me as odd that such a silly thing as attending a meeting could affect me so intensely. Finally, a wee bit of what I recalled from my Jungian studies managed to seep into my thoughts. A peculiar idea abruptly brought the recycling of my justifications to a halt: maybe, just maybe, *they* were not as greedy as I had been led to believe. Maybe greedy one was me? Perhaps I refused to go to the reading of Aunt Ellen's will because I couldn't stomach hearing *what I wasn't going to inherit!*

The Crushing Blow

The notion of greed carries with it such negativity that you might assume the recognition of my greedy nature might have been devastating, but you would be so wrong. The instant—I mean the very second—the belief I was greedy replaced my childhood prejudice, spirit pierced my awareness with raw, unconditional love, a sensation some might call bliss. The immediacy of this transformation was glorious. (Note: Spirit, when I spell it with a small s, refers to the universal spirit that unites us all. Capitalized, Spirit refers to God.)

In the space of a nanosecond, my perceptions radically switched. Love for my once abhorred aunts and cousins instantly replaced my prejudice. The transformation was so extreme that it was as if day had suddenly turned to night or black had converted to white. I was not the same person I was before. I was born anew.

Set in Stone

Aspects of the movie *The Truman Show* parallel this incident in several ways. If you recall, the movie is about a successful reality television show that began broadcasting every moment of Truman Burbank's life 24/7 shortly after his birth. The show hinges on the fact Truman remains ignorant of his circumstances: that millions have viewed his entire life as the feature of a television show. The show's producers rely on the supposition most people hold about the nature of their reality: that it is indisputable. They assume Truman will follow suit.

Had Truman not turned out to be a curious, highly intelligent boy, things might have remained fine and dandy, the show continuing as long as Truman lived. But that was not to be. Even in his youth, Truman realizes that aspects of his life do not add up. As he advances in years, so do his suspicions. Covertly, he goes about unearthing evidence to support his suspicions. As cleverly concealed as Truman thinks his investigations are, they do not go unnoticed; the producers are on to his antics. Colluding with the other actors to dissuade him, they believe their efforts to curb Truman's skepticism are successful, and to some extent, they are. However, inconsistencies keep arising to tickle Truman's suspicions. Truman becomes emboldened when he reaches adulthood.

Determined to unearth the truth about his life once and for all, Truman sets out on his sailboat on a balmy afternoon, presumably to enjoy a day on the water. All remains copacetic until Truman's true intent dawns on the producers. They go berserk. Thinking that if Truman fears for his life, he would return, they conjure up the fiercest storm clouds conceivable, which would deter most sailors, but not Truman. He suspects the storm is just another sham. He sails on. The producers become desperate. They rev up every special effect at their disposal, but again to no avail. Each attempt to escalate the peril only strengthens Truman's resolve to unearth the truth about his life. In the end, Truman blasts his boat through the walls of the television studio set and triumphantly emerges a free man.

Just as the premise of *The Truman Show* created a false identity for Truman, our childhood beliefs that are for the most part based on other peoples' opinions about who we are create the same type of identity for us. As they did with Truman, these identities limit our lives. The belief I was pure limited my life in the same way the beliefs the producers instilled in Truman limited his life. I truly felt like Truman must have when I blasted through the walls of the false reality and conflict my beliefs had created.

With this in mind my Pivotal Event raised questions that had never occurred to me before. What is the reality that my beliefs have forced upon me? Is this reality, like Truman's, an illusion? If it is, what reality is genuine? Even more to the point, how did the beliefs that my reality is based on develop—and as Truman began to question, are they real? By examining the details of my childhood, much of this became apparent.

Thoughts to Ponder

♦ Which of your parents' beliefs might you have adopted as a child?

♦ How do you feel about the idea that your reality might be an illusion?

Chapter 3

The Seeds of My Beliefs

I present the following autobiographical sketch for several reasons. First, the childhood experiences illustrate the environment that gave rise to why I began writing this book: the need to understand love and the ins and outs of our ability to love. Second, these experiences lay the groundwork for much of the theory I propose about beliefs as I use them to explain my ideas. Knowing them, I hope, will help make it easier for you to relate to the concept I am proposing. Finally, I hope my past will demonstrate that whatever ugly experiences life may have thrown in your path now generating conflict are fodder for healthy spiritual growth.

This story features a mother who could have been the poster child for narcissism, an emotionally repressed father, two "good" older siblings, one hysterical third child—me—and a Latvian maid with post-traumatic stress disorder (PTSD) from events that happened to her family during World War II.

Even though everyone is unique, human beings share certain universal feelings and desires, like the need to be loved and accepted. According to my family's perception, I was different. I was at the bottom of the heap in every conceivable way in what is known as the "black sheep" of my family.

My brother, being male, was the light of our parent's life; he could do no wrong. My petite sister took after Mother in size and personality, which made her acceptable—but not me. Having inherited my father's height, I was big. Most people naturally expect taller people to weigh more due to their height, but not Mother. The woman was obsessed with weight. When I was eight, she promised to buy me my first watch if I lost four pounds. The pounds came off, but the loss didn't change the fact that "I was not like them."

Dilemma

The blueprint for my parents' relationship was the 1940s notion of marriage: husband and wife slept in separate beds (á la Lucille Ball and Desi Arnez in their 1950s sitcom); Daddy went to work and provided for the family; Mother tended the home and children. I must have understood this arrangement because it never occurred to me to seek Daddy's counsel about how Agnes was treating me. Desperate, it finally dawned on me to beg Mother to tell Daddy about my plight, hoping he would rescue me. After repeatedly nagging her about this, Mother finally claimed to have told him; however, according to her, he told her to do what was best for her and that was that. Knowing what I do now, this is likely the truth. Daddy virtually worshiped Mother; he couldn't deny her anything.

Things might have been different if there had been someone on my side, someone who believed in me, perhaps a second-grade teacher or a close family friend, but there was never anyone.

In my mid-teens, the hopelessness of my situation finally became more than I was willing to bear. Being desperate to find relief, suicide seemed the most uncomplicated means of escape. After hearing about the lethal combination of alcohol and sleeping pills that caused the accidental death of a well-known television personality, I thought I'd found a way out. So, one night, I downed a glass of bourbon and swallowed a bottle of Mother's sleeping pills (which, oddly enough, she never mentioned missing). Clearly, it didn't work. The intake of so much alcohol proved too much for my stomach. Immediately, it revolted. Within minutes, up came the bourbon and with it, the pills, but not all. In the short time between the intake and the revolt, some pills began dissolving. Consequently, the following day, I slept until close to suppertime. No one took notice, even though it was a well-established fact that I was a morning person. More likely, no one dared question the anomaly. The answer would have put the family in an uncomfortable position.

After failing at suicide, I begged to see a psychiatrist. From the get-go, the request didn't stand a chance. Me spilling the beans to someone outside the family? Never! The consequences were too threatening; a shakeup of Mother's tidy life. It didn't help that my brother was dating the daughter of the only psychiatrist in town, not to mention that the family lived in our neighborhood. And, too, in the 1950s, if anyone knew I was seeing a psychiatrist, it was the social kiss of death. As Mother said, "We don't do such things." So, I remained under siege.

My Conditioning

Our family's situation captured the quintessence of the "good life"—Caucasian, Christian, and wealthy. So how could we have any problems? Situated on our monetary pedestal, we were cut off from the community at large, exempt from the scrutiny to which "lesser" families are subject. The assumption was, and maybe still is, that people who have money couldn't possibly have problems. Money solves all problems, yes? Encapsulated in our wealthy cocoon, a categorically unhealthy environment of emotional abuse flourished.

To be sure, there were advantages to growing up wealthy. I did, and still do, appreciate perks such as attending summer camps (which were a godsend), a private school education, and college. I enjoyed many of these despite the mortifying caveats sometimes accompanying them. According to one of my college professors, my grades didn't meet her college's standards. I was admitted only because the administration knew my father was wealthy. (Being ADD before attention deficit disorder was recognized, I gave in to my teachers' expectations and did little to dissuade them until I escaped their influence by going to college.) Continuing her litany, my professor said the administration knew that if the college ever needed money, they could always call on my father for help—as long as I was enrolled. You might think that after years of emotional abuse, I would no longer take notice of another pelting of negative comments, but no. I had learned not to complain despite the pain these remarks always caused.

When I was barely six, I was left alone, at the mercy of Mother's Latvian maid, Agnes. Tragically, my earlier and first "keeper," Nettie, conditioned me about what to expect from other "keepers." From when I was six months old until she left when I was about four, Nettie welcomed me into almost every aspect of her life, probably because she never had children. One memory from those times is of Nettie and her husband, Tucker, happily lounging around our kitchen table after eating lunch with the three of us children. Having observed Tucker spitting tobacco while working outside, it looked like he was spitting out chocolate or Coca-Cola. So, I asked him if I could try some. He gave me a chew. As my teeth sank into the tobacco, the disappointed expression on my face sent everyone choking with laughter.

The hours I spent with Nettie sitting on the kitchen counter, watching her cook, were the happiest of all. Lulled into a sleepy distraction listening to Lowell Thomas reporting the news, I watched as Nettie rolled out pie crusts and the like. As to the items in Nettie's closet, there was little doubt her shoes far surpassed Mother's for glamour. Nettie had five-inch high, open-toed, pseudo-alligator black patent leather shoes—trimmed, no less, with a ribbon of scarlet around the base of the soles! Be still my heart. The only shoes in Mother's closet that could compare were a pair of low-heeled pink satin bedroom slippers. Granted, the slippers were trimmed with rabbit fur dyed pink. They were pretty, but no match for the exotica I found in Nettie's closet.

If I were lucky, on her days off, Nettie would take me with her to some of the most fascinating places I never could have imagined. The one I liked the most was going to her trailer in the south end of town: a miniature house that contained incredibly wonderful smells. Then, there was her family farm in Waddy, Kentucky. There, you had to do your business in an outhouse, and even more exotic, you got to witness the spectacle of her father taking off his leg at night! Nothing like that ever happened at our house. It is sad to say that Tucker divorced Nettie, and soon after, Nettie had to leave Mother's employ, and she had to leave me. I not only lost Nettie, I lost wandering through our woods in the spring with her as she taught me the names of wildflowers and what wild greens to cut for supper, picnics watching the Ohio River's floodwaters rising, playing in the brook below our house, collecting watercress. Her absence left a huge void in my life. Over the years that followed, Nettie would drop by every so often for a visit. As I think about it now, the fact is that caring for me was just a job, but I didn't realize that at the time. All I knew was the only person I ever went to whenever I scraped my knee had disappeared.

It shocked us both when Agnes arrived to take over the care of the house, cooking, and me. While the job rescued Agnes and her enfeebled mother from further internment in German displaced person camps, I imagine in her eagerness to escape those abysmal conditions, the job description that specified caring for a small child, along with other duties, didn't wholly register in her mind. It was only when she and her sickly mother stepped off the train on that chilly November afternoon in 1949 and we came face-to-face did reality dawn.

Even when we first met, it was clear Agnes was not Nettie, but that didn't deter me. I was sure all my good-girl tricks that had worked so well in the past would win her over too. After all, I'd won over my much-feared neighbor's yard man, who Nettie claimed was Mr. McGregor, the villain in a childhood book, *Peter Rabbit*. It happened on a day when I was being particularly rowdy. Nettie dialed a number on Mother's pink Bakelite phone to keep me in line, pretending to be phoning Mr. McGregor for advice about handling me. To make amends, I sought out the yard man the next day and gave him a fistful of my best drawings, which seemed to have done the trick! Dumbfounded, the poor man returned a smile, the first I'd seen from him.

Agnes was always angry. The reason never varied: I wasn't like Latvian children. According to her, I was spoiled. Whatever that meant was never clear. It seemed the harder I tried the more callous Agnes became. Her forbidding presence in the kitchen, the one room I associated with comfort and love, became increasingly disturbing. Finally, on Valentine's Day, four months after Agnes and her mother took up residence in the wing of our house referred to as "the servants' quarters," she made her revulsion explicit.

Knowing that my pictures had won "Mr. McGregor's" heart, I was convinced that if I made a special valentine for Agnes and her mother, her heart would surely melt. She would embrace me and everything would return to normal. So, on that February morning, while Agnes was busy doing chores in the rest of the house, I snuck back to the servants' quarters and hung my very best valentines on the door to their rooms, one for Agnes and one for her mother. Anxious to see her smiling reaction, I waited in the kitchen for her return, sure that when she discovered my treasures, all would be forgiven, whatever that "all" was.

After Agnes returned to her rooms, hardly a second passed before she marched back into the kitchen. Red-faced, she flung the two valentines on the floor, and pronounced in her broken English, "I take nussing from you." But that wasn't true. Over the forty years or so that she worked for Mother, Agnes ripped out every psychologically healthy aspect from me—my self-esteem, my sense of power, of belonging. This wasn't hard. I was a sitting duck. If Nettie had not conditioned me to expect a close and loving relationship with my keeper, Agnes' expressions of revenge could never have made the impact they did. My relationship with Nettie left me craving human contact. I was desperate for the warmth and love I associated with the person in the kitchen that my mother could not give. Like a puppy who fulfills an instinctual need by chewing on everything in sight, I was a constant presence around Agnes.

In those days, people viewed psychiatry as dark, dangerous, and socially unacceptable. This meant someone who had suffered, as had Agnes, needed to find her own means to exorcise her demons or go insane. For this reason, I, who even in the best of circumstances Agnes would have regarded as a soggy, snotty handkerchief, became the intermediary by which she maintained her sanity. I was the enemy, the Russian soldiers who had brutally destroyed her family. Without question, she needed psychological help to deal with her traumas. Instead, through the way she treated me, she was able to restore her sense of power over her fate, avenging the monsters (I represented) who had destroyed her life.

My craving for human contact predisposed me to fall for Agnes' lures. If an obvious subject was not handy, Agnes discovered she could always draw me in by expressing interest in my life. Regardless of what came out of my mouth, she would pounce. Being masterful at gaslighting, she twisted my words like Chinese contortionists, wringing out all semblance of logic, and leaving me crying in frustration.

She had a knack for cleverly timing her attacks, so the height of my agitation exactly coincided with the entrance of one of my siblings. All anyone ever witnessed was a hysterical little Cathy on the kitchen floor, overwhelmed in tears, screaming at Agnes, with Agnes standing by, totally mystified. My reactions to her attacks turned me into the family pariah. This made Agnes' efforts all the sweeter. I became the blight of everyone's existence: Mother because my need for her attention interfered with the role she had adopted as the "lady of the house"; my brother and sister, Jay and Joyce, because, as long as I was the enemy, they could do little wrong; they were on the good team. I know my father loved me, but when doing something to help me meant going against his wife's wishes, he couldn't do it. As the tension in the house increased, he found callings in noble causes to keep him away from home most nights. Being a natural leader, at times Daddy was the head of the United Way, our church's vestry, the YMCA, as well as other organizations unknown to me at the time.

Details of Agnes' attacks are a blur because they happened daily. The memory that best captures the essence of this period is the sequence of events that occurred when a grade-school friend of mine came to spend the night. When we were called to dinner, without a preamble, Mother did something she'd never done before, or, for that matter, ever did again. She invited Marion to sit at the table at my customary place next to her.

This abrupt disruption in the usual order threw me off balance. Instantly, Agnes picked up on my distress. It offered her the perfect opening. As she went around the table serving vegetables, I glanced up at her. The deep satisfaction that beamed over Agnes' face was too much: she had hit her mark spot-on. I exploded in tears of anger. This reaction exceeded her expectations. It was the first of only two instances in my life when, for appearances only, Mother felt forced to take action. She ordered me to go to the back hall to wait out what she called my histrionics.

This exile presented Agnes with a situation that was too choice to ignore. Having to pass by me when she returned to the kitchen, she couldn't help herself. Whispering carefully selected words of triumph as she passed by me sent me over the top. The next thing I knew, I was running up the stairs with Mother beating my legs with a fly swatter. While the incident ended my friendship with Marion, it gave Mother a mantra she used from then on: "Cathy is such a problem; I just don't know what to do with her." Those words kept unconsciously echoing in my head throughout my childhood and the early years of my adulthood.

Yup, the bane of everyone's existence, that was me, or I should say, it was the identity that their opinions of me trapped me into believing about myself. Their beliefs had nothing to do with me as a person. They only served to justify how they treated me. Strangely enough, somewhere in the recesses of my mind I sensed the wrongness of these accusations, but their unwavering attitudes outweighed any thoughts I had to the contrary.

Mother's stolid indifference toward my situation left me naked to Agnes' wiles. I probably exaggerate how often I told Mother about my predicament, but it seems I made an attempt every other week. These confrontations occurred in the afternoons as Mother was dressing for dinner. Sitting on the pink taffeta stool in front of her dressing table, I sobbed, pleading with her to fire Agnes because she was so cruel to me. Even if I exaggerate the frequency of this scenario, no matter. There is no question that Mother was well-informed about my plight.

I suspect, on some level, Mother knew she needed to do something about Agnes, but she just couldn't bring herself to do it. When Mother gave dinner parties, guests often complimented her on how lucky she was to have Agnes, *a white woman,* working for her. It was apparent Mother's need for admiration took precedence over my well-being. Her awareness of my plight insinuated itself more and more into her opinion of me. Based on how her heart seemed to hardened towards me, I suspect awareness of her duplicity forced Mother to find ways to rationalize her behavior so that she could keep betraying me. Any success I had flew in the face of the problematic child she purported me to be. Whenever I excelled at something, she treated it as a personal offense. Consequently, I became her enemy.

As a teenager I began writing as a way to vent my outrage. I must have spewed my anger through countless reams of paper—always immediately destroying these shameful confessions. Often, after one of these writing rampages, I would write poems. During my senior year in high school, I served on the yearbook committee. At one of our meetings, I learned that the number of entries for the highly coveted literary award was abysmally low. I submitted one of my poems only to fatten the file, never expecting anyone would take notice. However, at our last meeting, just as the yearbook went to press, I learned I'd won the contest—me, the blight of my teachers' existence: I'd won *the* literary contest.

Such an achievement would thrill most parents, but not Mother. The woman even refused to read the poem. She ignored all attempts to share my triumph with her. The achievement was so outstanding I wasn't about to let her get away with her lack of acknowledgement. So, I insisted on reading it to her. With catatonic indifference she kept her eyes riveted on her knitting. Obviously, my achievement didn't comply with the person her justifications had turned me into. As long as I was a failure, Mother could keep treating me as a problem, but being publicly heralded as a winner—even by her friends at church no less—threatened to bankrupt her negative opinions of me that were so necessary to preserve in order for her to save face.

Mother's refusal to protect me served as a silent blessing on Agnes' behavior, giving her carte blanche over me.

Agnes could treat me however she pleased, and no one raised an eyebrow. Abandoned in hostile territory, with the enemy continually lurking, waiting to attack, there was no one I could go to for help or a place of safety except for the attic or the woods surrounding our house. Being barely six years old when the mistreatment began, I was too young to understand the futility of any response. Agnes' accusations were never meant to be logical. The whole point of her gaslighting was to bamboozle me, and could she ever! No matter how much I tried telling Mother, Jay, or Joyce what had happened, no one would listen to a child, especially a hysterical one.

These repeated failures convinced me I was incapable of defending myself. I was not only unworthy of being protected, but incapable of doing it myself.

One incident I remember clearly illustrates my family's attitude towards me. It happened on an afternoon when my brother was expected home from college. When Agnes saw his car coming around the driveway, with just enough time to sow whatever words she knew would bring me to tears, she struck. Just as the results of her attack were coming to fruition, to my great relief, I heard Jay's footsteps on the staircase coming up from the garage. As he entered the kitchen, I ran to him, begging him to help me. His response: he calmly ordered me to go to my room, reiterating the refrain I had heard chorused so often, "Poor Agnes, she has suffered so much."

Within those enameled yellow steel walls of our kitchen, I endured—a David without a slingshot facing a Goliath, symbolic of all the injustices ever committed against Agnes and her family. But now, each encounter with the enemy left her triumphful. Never again was Agnes the victim as she had been in Latvia. Abandoned in the wilderness, I shouldered the blame for everyone's problems. I adopted their noxious accusations even though, in truth, their opinions were not about me, only how they saw me. Nevertheless, unconsciously, my identity came to reflect the person they believed me to be. Something about me was wrong.

Ironically, all this transpired in one of the most architecturally exquisite houses in Louisville, Kentucky, at the time. Very few people outside the family had any idea about the toxic atmosphere within—at least, as far as I knew. Much later, a few people admitted they suspected something had been amiss, but they never spoke up for me when I was a child, much less raised the issue with Mother.

When I was about ten years old, I clearly remember apologizing to God for having been born.

The Final Straw

With my siblings away in college, interactions with Agnes continued along a well-established pattern: Agnes needing retribution by heaping mortifications on me, and I, in turn, emotionally fracturing. That is, until one afternoon when the level of Agnes's malevolence reached a particularly potent high. Added to years of unrelenting verbal flogging, the venom she released on me that day outstripped my endurance. With nowhere to go, no one to help, and every trace of hope pounded out of me, nothing was left to hold onto.

Years of stifled rage erupted.

At one point, Agnes knelt down to pick something off the kitchen floor. Spotting a knife on the cutting board, I grabbed it and held it above her head. I don't know what I intended. I just wanted relief—to shut her up, stop the spewing of her distorted accusations. Sensing something amiss, Agnes looked up. For the first and only time, we bonded in tears: hers due to the horror of seeing me holding a knife over her head, mine by the jolt of recognizing the extent of my rage that made me do such an unconscionable thing. Making me promise never to tell anyone about what had happened, Agnes let up on me for a short while.

I complied with Agnes' request, but she needn't have worried. I could barely face my own thoughts about the episode, much less confess what I'd done to anyone. The whole thing was too appalling. If I had had even a trace of positive self-esteem before the event, the all-consuming state of shame and guilt that engulfed me afterward would have shredded it. Never again did I need to be reminded that I was a reprehensibly disgusting human being. My actions that day were proof: 'they' had been right all along.

Not long after, the pressure from her demons made continued assaults mandatory. And so ended the truce. And it never stopped. Even after I married and had children, Agnes maintained her Machiavellian behavior towards me.

When I was about thirty years old, I finally sought the help of a psychiatrist. He became the first person I had ever entrusted with the details of my past. After several stays in a psychiatric hospital and weekly therapy sessions, three years later, I married Ken.

Because I wanted to start our life without the gloom of my past hovering over me, I decided to leave therapy in the hope I could cut myself off from memories of my childhood. When I informed my doctor of this decision, he accused me of making up my past. In keeping with his Freudian background, he insisted the stories I'd told him about my childhood were so outrageous, I must have fabricated them—but of course, he added, I did it for a good reason. After all, it seemed to him I had escaped relatively unscathed. Talk about adding insult to injury! This accusation from the first person I had ever entrusted with the secrets of my heart couldn't have hurt me more.

How I managed to survive eluded me too. From what I know now, the roots of my salvation probably rested in the first four years of my life when Nettie was my keeper. The love and companionship between us nurtured me in a way every child deserves. Even so, shame and guilt over the knife incident took years for me to overcome. The conflict it left in its wake fashioned the box of my reality—locking me into significantly damaged beliefs about my identity. The lessons I learned from the Pivotal Event about the quixotic nature of beliefs have helped me break through my box as Truman did when he crashed his boat through the television set. In the same way Truman's knowledge of his background armed him with the will to reveal the truth, however, this knowledge alone got him only so far. the difficulty of unearthing a problematic belief can be highly challenging.

Conflict can give you the desire to understand the origins of your beliefs, but the many unconscious aspects comprising a belief can be so devious and deceptive, in order to break out of your box it is necessary to arm yourself with knowledge of these facets and how they affect your behavior.

First, I need to introduce you to the origin of the concept I believe to be fundamental to our beliefs, the nature of our reality, and, as a consequence, the feature inhibiting spiritual growth.

Thoughts to Ponder

◆ Everyone grows up with a childhood tale to tell; most, I suspect, are far worse than mine. Writing a brief account of yours may help identify problematic beliefs.

◆ Had you lived my childhood, what beliefs might you hold about yourself now?

Part II

The Human Foundation

Chapter 4

The Dawn of Fear

I suspect every translation of the Bible contains the same weighty words found in the second and third chapters of Genesis that chronicle Adam and Eve's life in Paradise. According to tradition, Adam and Eve's actions described in these verses affected their future and, purportedly, all of humanity's thereafter.

Innumerable books and articles have been written about these two chapters of Genesis. The most noteworthy recent one to appear is by Bill Moyers, *Genesis, A Living Conversation*. In this tome, several erudite scholars explore the meaning of the words as they reflect our *current perception* of reality. By scrutinizing these verses through the lens of psychology, however, unrecognized forces come to light. This approach offers a potential for humanity to grow spiritually in ways never before imagined by eliminating conflict.

The perception of God that the traditional interpretation of Adam and Eve's story left us with is so familiar that it may as well be inscribed in our DNA: a god who oversees, punishes and judges every action. This characterization contradicts the notion of an unconditionally loving god.

For people who might not be acquainted with Adam and Eve's story, recounting the details of their saga as they appear in the Book of Bereishit (Genesis) from the Jewish Virtual Library[4] will help me explain my hypothesis. Beginning with Genesis 2:7:

> And the LORD God formed man of the dust of the ground, and breathed into his nostrils the breath of life; and man became a living soul.

God then tells Adam, he can eat freely of every tree, but in Genesis 2:16-17, imposes limitations:

> And the LORD God commanded the man, saying, Of every tree of the garden thou mayest freely eat: But of the tree of the knowledge of good and evil, thou shalt not eat of it: for in the day that thou tasteth thereof thou shalt surely die.

Continuing with Genesis 2:21-22:

> And the LORD God caused a deep sleep to fall upon Adam, and he slept: and he took one of his ribs, and closed up the flesh instead thereof; And the rib, which the LORD God had taken from man, made he a woman, and brought her unto the man.

> And they were both naked, the man and his wife, and were not ashamed.

Then, God leaves Adam and Eve alone in the garden. During God's absence, Adam and Eve disobey their father and eat of the forbidden tree. Their story continues in Genesis 3:7-10:

> And the eyes of them both were opened, and they knew that they were naked; and they sewed fig leaves together, and made themselves aprons.

And they heard the voice of the LORD God walking in the garden in the cool of the day: and Adam and his wife hid themselves from the presence of the LORD God amongst the trees of the garden. And the LORD God called unto Adam, and said unto him, Where art thou? And he said, I heard thy voice in the garden, *and I was afraid* [my emphasis] because I was naked; and I hid myself.

Considering we have been told (maybe a recent statement) that God is omniscient, we already know he knows they have disobeyed him; nevertheless, he confronts them in Genesis 3:11-13:

And he said, Who told thee that thou wast naked? Hast thou eaten of the tree, whereof I commanded thee that thou shouldest not eat? And the man said, The woman whom thou gavest to be with me, she gave me of the tree, and I did eat. And the LORD God said unto the woman, What is this that thou hast done? And the woman said, The serpent beguiled me, and I did eat.

In the following verses of 3:14-23, God's pronouncements contradict how he was initially portrayed.

And the LORD God said unto the serpent, Because thou hast done this, thou art cursed above all cattle, and above every beast of the field; upon thy belly shalt thou go, and dust shalt thou eat all the days of thy life: And I will put enmity between thee and the woman, and between thy seed and her seed; it shall bruise thy head, and thou shalt bruise his heel. Unto the woman he said, I will greatly multiply thy sorrow and thy conception; in sorrow thou shalt bring forth children; and thy desire shall be to thy husband, and he shall rule over thee. And unto Adam he said, Because thou hast hearkened unto the voice of thy wife, and hast eaten of the tree, of which I commanded thee, saying, Thou shalt not eat of it: cursed is the ground for thy sake; in sorrow shalt thou eat of it all the days of thy life; Thorns also and thistles shall it bring forth to thee; and thou shalt eat the herb of the field; In the sweat of thy face shalt thou eat bread, till thou return unto the ground; for out of it wast thou taken: for dust thou art, and unto dust shalt thou return. And Adam called his wife's name Eve; because she was the mother of all living. Unto Adam also and to his wife did the LORD God make coats of skins, and clothed them. And the LORD God said, Behold, the man is become as one of us, to know good and evil: and now, lest he put forth his hand, and take also of the tree of life, and eat, and live for ever: Therefore, the LORD God sent him forth from the Garden of Eden, to till the ground from whence he was taken.

The shift in these verses from God as the epitome of all-encompassing, unconditional love to an angry father figure who smites and punishes naughty human beings is quite dramatic. This characterization pretty much continues through the entire Old Testament. I suspect our Biblical forefathers who authored those words had never experienced God as he was initially portrayed—an unconditionally loving father. The only example of a father I imagine they had was their own: someone who determined good from bad and ruled accordingly. Not only that, everyone knew you had to please your father, abide by his rules, or suffer punishment. But a god who loved you regardless of what you did was beyond their ability to conceive. On the other hand, they could relate to a heavenly father who mirrored their experiences with their parents—an angry God (parent) who determined good from bad and accordingly leveled punishments. Thus, they never questioned the muddled perception of this heavenly father that these verses portray—the version of God that Hebrews, Muslims, and Christians first embraced and sadly still do.

A psychological interpretation of these events liberates this concept from the idea of an angry God that judges. The loving Creator from the first chapter of Genesis reappears.

Thoughts to Ponder

♦ When you first heard or read the account of Adam and Eve, did the idea of a serpent being able to talk strike you as odd?

♦ How has the idea of a God who smites and punishes naughty human beings affected you?

♦ If you accepted the idea that God loves you regardless of who you are or what you do, how would that affect you?

♦ How would that change your behavior, your thoughts?

Chapter 5

A Psychological Interpretation

During my Pivotal Event, upon discovering the unconscious role fear played in supporting my prejudice, I found striking parallels between what happened to Adam and Eve and what happened to me. This revelation seeded the premise of my theory.

Beginning with Genesis 2, after God creates Adam and Eve, God and his offspring are fully aware of each other and freely interact. During this time, God brings Adam the beasts and fowl of the Earth to name and warns him against eating the fruit from a particular tree. It is an idyllic world in which the human heart, mind, and spirit operate as one—in unity with God: the acme of spiritual perfection.

Then, the story takes a turn. One morning, God tells his children he is leaving the house for the day; perhaps he tells them he is going out to run a few errands. Before departing, he again reminds his offspring not to eat the fruit from the forbidden tree.

This warning could not have given these two youngsters a more compelling reason to investigate. Outlawing the fruit has only enhanced its allure. Having had children, I can see these two putting their heads together and speculating about this fruit they have been told contains strange properties. Really? Seeing the tree's branches arching, heavy with fruit, the idea occurs to both almost simultaneously: there are so many fruits; if they ate just one, there's no way their father could miss it. So, they do the big *IT* and disobey their father. (Okay, this act reportedly involved a serpent tempting Eve to disobey their father: an idea that served the original interpreter's level of understanding. For my purposes, it exposes the crux of the story, as I will be explaining.)

A short while later, their father returns only to find his children are nowhere in sight. God calls out to Adam and asks him where he is. Adam comes out of hiding and replies in Genesis 3:10, "I heard thy voice in the garden, *and I was afraid,* because I was naked; and I hid myself." At this juncture, several incongruities stand out.

Let's be honest; you don't have to be God to know they did the big *IT.* Any adult, parent or not, could tell Adam and Eve ate the fruit. By merely observing Adam and Eve's behavior the truth is obvious. Nevertheless, God keeps interacting with his children through fourteen more verses as if it were just another day in Paradise! If I had been a newspaper reporter writing a headline about the state of affairs at that moment, it might read: **"Disobedient Children Still Enjoy Spiritual Perfection."**

The most striking aspect is *what doesn't happen*: there is no immediate punishment. While disobedience introduces Adam and Eve to the fact that fear exists (knowledge of good and evil) and the recognition that their bodies are different, these two revelations pretty much sum up the consequences of their actions.

Think about it. The present lack of punishment and their continued interactions with their father for a few minutes (or verses) more is most peculiar. God knows they ate the fruit, yet there is no mention that he punishes the miscreants as you might expect—especially *if disobedience* is the matter of contention. What God does do is ask them *if* they disobeyed him—but once again, God is omniscient! Why would this all-knowing father ask his children if they ate the forbidden fruit, knowing they did? Nothing suggests the father lost his senses while out running errands. The fact that God asks his children if they disobeyed him indicates to me that more is going on than words alone indicate. Nevertheless, he asks, and *they answer.*

Upon their replies, we read everything God declares and does dramatically changes. The depiction of God changes to the extent that it contradicts everything about the way he was earlier portrayed. Beginning with Genesis 3:14-17, this unconditionally loving father appears to have metamorphosed into another being. If you had only begun reading Genesis at verse 3:14, this father, whose words now appear may as well be a human father, not God as he initially appears.

Understandably, early analysts had no cause to question the peculiar disposition of God's query. Nor did they take issue with the implausibility of Adam and Eve's bizarre answers. Instead, they focused on aspects they could relate to: Adam and Eve hiding their genitalia while ignoring the puzzling elements, such as Eve's excuse for disobeying her father's mandate which is about as strange as it gets—a snake with the ability *to talk* lured her into eating the forbidden fruit. Inexperience may have made these analysts open to accommodating any reason Eve might have given. Perhaps what happened to them was like what happened to me when my parents took me to movies with adult content: anything I couldn't relate to went right over my head.

In light of what these analysts knew, the cause and effect of Adam and Eve's plight was simple: some undefined factor caused these two youngsters to disobey their father, and eviction was their punishment. Given what was known at the time, these conclusions make sense. Lacking a better way to account for Adam and Eve's assumed expulsion from Eden, they decided some sort of innate flaw in Adam and Eve made them disobey their father, which they labeled, calling the flaw—sin.

This interpretation and the bizarre characterization of God in human terms thereafter continues throughout the Old Testament. This unfortunate portrayal prevails in most religious communities today. The idea that their Creator loves unconditionally, as Genesis 2 portrays, baffled them in the same way my dream's message confounded me.

Viewed Through a Psychology Lens

Examining these verses through the lens of psychology, when Adam admits to being afraid, it is apparent disobedience has *introduced* Adam and Eve to the fact that fear exists. At this juncture, fear is something they have just been introduced to on the order of grass is green, the sun rises and sets every day, and bears poop in the woods, as well as knowledge of good and evil. Despite their newfound *awareness* of fear, Adam and Eve's relationship with their father remains steadfast—despite the fact they have just disobeyed him and he knows it. As attested by their continued relationship with their father, unconditional love continues to govern their perception of reality as it has from the moment of their inception. Simultaneously then, Adam and Eve are aware of fear while unconditional love governs their perception of reality. At this juncture fear remains *inert:* a mere awareness.

Then, their father questions them.

I imagine God would have forgiven them if Adam and Eve had admitted they ate the forbidden fruit, like most loving parents. Then, making each promise never to do it again, this father would have sent them out to name a couple of newly created insects or some such thing. Knowledge of good and evil aside, the problem would have ended there *if* the story was intended to illustrate the depth and breadth of God's unconditional love, which forgiveness would have borne out. But the story is not about God nor his love.

A psychological examination of Genesis 3:10-24 alludes to a clue similar in effect to the one Dan Brown used in his work of fiction, *The Da Vinci Code.* Dan Brown based this book on the idea that Leonardo da Vinci left a clue to a greater truth in his famous painting of the Last Supper. As with *The Da Vinci Code,* a psychological examination of Genesis 3 exposes a different reality that elucidates the presence of Adam and Eve's story.

Here, the clue resides in the single word: *afraid.* Once I understood the role *unconscious* fear played in my Pivotal Event, a completely different interpretation of Adam and Eve's "fall" occurred to me. In light of what I deduced about how fear *unconsciously* emotionally affected me, I realized disobedience had little to do with Adam and Eve's supposed fall and subsequent eviction. The cause of this dramatic change was something else entirely.

According to traditional interpretations, disobedience exposes the fact that Adam and Eve, whom God created in his image, were created as flawed beings. Wait—flawed beings created in God's image? The idea defies logic. If God is perfect and he created Adam and Eve in his own image, logically, this would suggest Adam and Eve must be perfect, too. But not according to the traditional interpretation. They, as well as we, are supposedly broken beings in a broken world, always and forever—an interpretation that has been the leading rationalization for the human condition. As a precept, this explanation has served religions well, giving believers a reason that explains the existence of conflict, the root of human suffering. Its true genius, however, is only now coming to light. Untutored, we have missed its brilliance. Until now, Augustine's interpretation of Original Sin has been the leading, singular explanation for Adam and Eve's plight.

A psychological analysis of the effects of the word "afraid" suggests a more comprehensive reason for what has been interpreted as Adam and Eve's "fall." And with that, the hope for humanity teeters.

The Clue Plays Out

Since fear is the antithesis of love, the appearance of fear in Paradise is decidedly alien. Love defines Paradise. The inconsistency of fear's presence in Paradise emphasizes its preternatural occurrence. If Adam and Eve had remained simply aware of fear, these two immaculate clones of their father might have lingered in Paradise forever, mini-gods playing hide-and-seek in their father's garden. And too, had this happened when you think about it, there might never have been an "us" had fear not entered the picture, especially when you consider the later verse in Genesis 3:16 about painful childbirth. Even though they recognize differences in their bodies, without fear, Adam and Eve, innocent and indifferent to their sexuality, could easily have remained chaste and, therefore, childless. Thus, no "us," period.

So, what is it about Adam and Eve's answers that begs a different interpretation?

These verses begin with Adam blaming Eve for making him eat the fruit, and then Eve blames a serpent for talking her into disobeying their father's edict. Psychologically speaking, the very nature of their replies indicates an unknown element has entered their minds and has caused a change of epic proportions. The fact their answers rely on *blame* reveals this cataclysmic change. In lawyer-speak, a psychological analysis of blame is dispositive evidence; in other words, it is unequivocal proof that the nature of fear has transformed. No longer a dormant awareness as it first appeared, fear has now become unconsciously *activated.* In this unconscious state it can function as an *operational* force. From this point on, operational fear begins generating emotions that unconsciously affect Adam and Eve's perceptions. The way Adam and Eve understand their life and surroundings radically switches. The unconscious impact from emotions *distorts* their perceptions, affecting everything Eve and Adam think and do thereafter.

It is no small coincidence when fear turns operational, we read that God's character dramatically changes. This once unconditionally loving father turns into an angry God who curses the snake as well as his children. Not only that, it seems you can actually displease this transmuted God, and when you do, you will be punished.

The dramatic turn in God's posture alone supports this interpretation. Why? God cannot change. God is the epitome of unconditional love. God loves, period. Father Greg Boyle, in his book *Tattoos on the Heart,* aptly characterizes how God loves as the "whateverness" of God, saying, "God is just so busy loving us to have any time left for disappointment." [5] This father never judges. He loves without qualifications of any sort. Until blame enters the picture, life seemed to be copacetic. However, upon Adam and Eve's answers, in all of a nanosecond, this loving father's character reportedly changes, flips upside down and backward. Based on the jarring nature of God's words in verses 3:17-19 denouncing his children illustrates a remarkable transformation in God. These verses suggest that if there was a "fall," it occurred *after* Adam and Eve answer him.

If God cannot change what is the source of this variant depiction of him? Based on my experiences with fear, the source of this alien depiction lies in the way operational fear has begun affecting them, distorting their perceptions. God doesn't change. Only Adam and Eve's perception of God changes. Their newly altered fear-based perceptions are the source of this transformed portrayal of God.

Understandably, given what happens at the end of Genesis 3, early analysts never questioned the peculiarity of God asking Adam and Eve *if* they disobeyed him. In light of what these scholars knew, the cause and effect of the children's plight was simple. Some factor within Adam and Eve's character caused them to disobey their father. Eviction was their punishment.

Religions still rely on this interpretation to justify human suffering. But think about it. How could these two beings, created in God's image and alive with the breath of God, be innately flawed? The logical inference would be that God is also imperfect.

Parallels That Expose the Story's Intent

The similarities between my Pivotal Event and Adam and Eve's experience were more than remarkable. In all *of a nanosecond,* the basis of *both* Adam and Eve's perceptions, as well as mine, spun 180 degrees around. It was like someone flipped the switch controlling our perceptions. With one major exception, the results were identical: *they occurred in reverse order.*

The moment I released my fear-based prejudice and adopted a love-based belief, symbolically white belief, my perception of reality switched from the black reality based on fear that I had known all my life to a white one founded in love. This rapid transformation in my awareness of spirit's love was riveting. It was as if in an instant my heart was born anew. It was obvious. The absence of fear initiated my Pivotal Event.

Based on this, I concluded that the only obstacle separating me from direct awareness of spirit is fear. Fear not only obscures my awareness of spirit, but based on experience it is the filter through which I initially perceive all life.

Adam and Eve's experience was the exact reverse. Coming from a world immersed in unconditional love, or symbolically white, when they answer God, their replies that rely on blame demonstrate that their perceptions have transformed. From that moment on, once fear becomes an unconscious, operational force in their minds, they can only perceive the black, fear-based reality I first knew.

The Impact of Adam and Eve's Switch

Once fear turns operational, it gives Adam and Eve the means to *function* as human beings.

The verses leading to this conclusion begin in Genesis 1:27; "So God created man in his own image." Having been created as beings of spirit, if Adam and Eve were ever going to be able to function as mortals, logically, everything about their lives would have to change. Had they not done the deed and eaten of the forbidden fruit, Adam and Eve would have remained innocent, chaste beings of spirit forever after according to Genesis 2:25; "And they were both naked, the man and his wife, and were not ashamed." It is only after they start blaming each other for disobeying their father we told in Genesis 3:16 they might have the interest and ability to procreate as human beings.

God's warning in Genesis 2:16 against eating the forbidden fruit foreshadows this pending transformation, "[F]or in the day that thou eatest thereof *thou shalt surely die* (my emphasis.)." Spirits do not die; they are eternal, infinite. At the time of this pronouncement, even though Adam, and later Eve, purportedly had bodies, it would seem that as beings of spirit they were not subject to death. Death occurs only to human beings.

The moment blame changes the nature of fear, it is apparent Adam and Eve's perception of fear as a mere awareness has changed as well as their perception of everything around them. Symbolically, the white world of unconditional love they initially knew has switched to black, the reality that fear generates when it turns operational as an unconscious force. The activation of fear constitutes Adam and Eve's conversion from beings of spirit to mortal human beings. For the first time, the *illusion* that most humans recognize today as reality is now theirs. The introduction of blame in the third book of Genesis is the clue, as in *The Da Vinci Code,* to the greater truth found in our creation story.

What is commonly recognized as their *"fall"* was the moment Adam and Eve's *perceptions* transformed, giving beings of spirit the ability to function as human beings.

The premise of my theory about spiritual growth relies on understanding and appreciating how fear impacts our brains. In particular, as an operational force, fear has the means by which it can control our behavior unconsciously. During my Pivotal Event, without knowing it, once I became aware of the fear that had been supporting the prejudice, the outgrown belief vanished. Once awareness supplanted unconscious fear, the operational aspect that had been sustaining the prejudice vanished. A new belief grounded in love then replaced the prejudice. Straightaway, a clear, unadulterated awareness of my spirit materialized: no fear, belief, resistance, emotion—nothing left to blind me to the perception of spirit.

Rendering fear a mere awareness decommissions operational fear. The barrier of unconscious fear evaporates. This allows our brains to perceive the essence of spirit and experience the "white" world Adam and Eve originally knew.

Thoughts to Ponder

♦ How does this conclusion affect the Old Testament's portrayal of an angry, punishing God?

♦ How do you feel about Father Greg Boyle's characterization of God as being "...just so busy loving us to have any time left for disappointment," in particular, the suggestion that God never judges?

♦ If God isn't judging us, who is?

♦ What do people gain by judging?

♦ If Adam and Eve's "fall" was not a fall, but something necessary for them to begin functioning as human beings, does sin still exist?

♦ How does this interpretation impact the concept of Original Sin?

Chapter 6

Fear

Essential to Functioning as a Human Being

The workshop I attended on fear mentioned in Chapter 6, which I initially thought was unrelated to either my dream or the Pivotal Event, ended up serving as the catalyst that resolved both my dream and the Pivotal Event. The resolution emerged by applying the information I acquired studying Jungian psychology to these topics. While the resulting account is speculative, it is grounded in my real-life experiences.

The Basis

Beginning sometime in infanthood, at a time when you are incapable of protecting yourself, I imagine fear serves as a type of psychological parent that exists to emotionally protect you. Let's say you are, say, ten months old. An unfamiliar person reaches out to take you from the safety of your mother's arms. You naturally draw back in fear. Perfect. A perceived upheaval in your life has just been averted, but that's only the beginning of the way fear functions as a psychological parent.

Overcome with fear at such a young age, raw vulnerability makes you unable to handle the emotions that inevitably accompany fear. Being susceptible to emotional overwhelm, continued submergence in fear and its emotions might put your survival in question. You could drown, thus, no more you. Fortunately, the way fear works as your psychological parent affecting your brain, it prevents this from happening.

The moment your brain detects fear, it separates you from awareness of fear. Lacking a better way to put it, your brain erects something on the order of an invisible wall. The purpose of this wall is to separate you not only from awareness of fear, but more importantly, the emotions that accompany it. The result; a catastrophe has just been avoided. As helpful as this is, the wall creates another problem: it leaves a destabilizing vacuum in your brain. In order to rebalance itself, the brain fills the vacuum by conjuring up a reason *why* the fear-producing event happened in the first place. Your current level of understanding determines the substance of the reason. Later, when you acquire words, you recognize these reasons as beliefs. The initiating fear still exists, just hidden from awareness, having been incorporated into the belief. All you remember is the belief.

By replacing the fear and its emotions with a belief, it could be said *fear* saved your life by generating a *belief.* Because your psyche equates your fear-generated beliefs with saving your life, it equates your beliefs as being your *life—your actual body.* Therefore, it treats your *beliefs* as if they are your *existence*—the compliment being, lose a belief, and you die.

As life evolves, new fears keep popping up. For each new fear that appears, the brain conjures up a reason to explain its existence. You recognize these reasons beliefs. Once a belief replaces a fear that your brain perceives as threatening, your awareness of it disappears. The fear still exists, just unconsciously. Now hidden behind the belief, it begins functioning operationally as a way to protect your life from emotional overwhelm that awareness of fear initially posed. Later, when faced with a situation that had elicited a fear your psyche recognizes, as your psychological parent, operational fear interjects itself into your present awareness. Immediately, it elicits resistance for the purpose of generating an emotion. Impacted by emotion you react or behave in a way that prevents you from proceeding with an activity that threatens to damage the belief (your life) in question, which would reveal the fear supporting it. As an example, when we are faced with an issue that unconsciously threatens a belief, resistance can cause us dig our heels in and refuse to think differently about an issue when everyone else readily accepts it.

The biggest challenge to spiritual growth is the erroneous, unconscious assumption, "lose a belief, and you die." You may grow up, but your psyche does not. According to your psyche, you are always the child you were when it began psychologically parenting you. Therefore, your childhood or basic beliefs remain as they originated, that is, unless you choose to change them. As an adult, without changing your childhood beliefs, you resort to reacting as you did as a child.

Because it was unconscious, the belief that I was not greedy naturally followed me into adulthood. However, as an adult, my security needs changed. They no longer relied on parental acceptance. Even though going against the family grain was not the threat it had been when I was a child, the lack of awareness perpetuated the family prejudice. With the unconscious fear still operable, I refused to attend the meeting that involved my aunt's will. Once I became aware that I was indeed greedy and accepted that aspect of my nature, awareness eliminated the *unconscious* aspect of the fear that had attached me to the prejudice. A love-based belief about my aunts then emerged, replacing the prejudice. An all-consuming feeling of bliss exploded, leaving me thunderstruck.

In my attempt to understand this mystical experience, I realized the moment I accepted my greedy nature, operational fear ceased working. My newfound awareness of the reason I had held on to the prejudice supplanted the fear. No longer needed to protect me from acknowledging this fear, awareness eliminated the need for my psychological parents' continuance. The three things that resulted established the foundation for my hypothesis. First, awareness eliminated my long-time prejudice against my aunts and cousins; the superior person that fear had unconsciously led me to think I was disappeared; and finally, based on the bliss that immediately followed, I concluded the absence of operational fear allowed my mind to open to direct awareness of my spirit.

Once I understood the psychological aspects that block awareness of spirit/love, I could repeat the steps. Eventually, this knowledge formed the basis of the type of spiritual growth I am proposing.

The Endgame

Eliminating the *unconscious* aspect of fear closely resembled what happened to the character of Truman when he blasted through the television set that had been encapsulating his life. By escaping the wall of beliefs that the show's producers had imposed on him, Truman discovered the truth about his existence. The truth of my existence also lay on the other side of my wall of fear-based beliefs: all that exists is love.

In the mind of this good Christian girl, the idea that there could be a psychological way to grow spiritually seemed outrageous; nevertheless, I could not deny what I had experienced. Switching to a love-based belief stripped fear of its need to keep protecting me. The invisible wall fear had created in my childhood brain as it pertained to the prejudice, collapsed. The absence of the wall allowed the perception of spirit to flood my senses. Considering that love is the antithesis of fear, this encounter made sense.

This discovery permitted me to develop a practical process of spiritual growth. Practical, because the process can be used anytime, anywhere, as the need arises; practical because it doesn't involve years of isolation in a far-off cave, or hours chanting "Om" as I had previously imagined.

As I define it, spiritual growth is a matter of expanding the ability to love unconditionally—not as human beings currently understand love, which unbeknownst to us is fear-based, but love as spirit loves— love with no conditions or judgments attached. Awareness of spirit expands in direct proportion to the absence of the operational or unconscious aspect of fear.

The idea that an unspecified issue separates us from spirit is very real. For centuries, the name assigned to that something has been "sin." In my experience, the toxic implications of sin negate the hope of ever mending that separation. Discoveries in the 21st century offer a productive rationale for mending that estrangement.

Understanding the basis of our beliefs and how they affect us allows us to take the necessary steps to completely reconcile our relationship with spirit.

Thoughts to Ponder

♦ Has a sudden realization ever dawned on you that made you feel you blasted through a wall of beliefs like Truman in the film *The Truman Show?*

♦ What are your current beliefs about how to grow spiritually?

♦ How do you feel about the notion of a psychological form of spiritual growth?

♦ How do your religious roots or current understanding of spirit differ?

Chapter 7

The Anatomy of a Belief

Rendering fear inoperable is the key to eliminating conflict and reconciling our relationship with spirit. It is a process based on a clear understanding of how fear unconsciously operates as it impacts our beliefs and, therefore, our behaviors.

Many people find the idea that fear underlies their beliefs disturbing. In the early 1990s, after I gave one of my workshops on unconscious fear and how it blocks our heart's desires, a participant approached me. The woman told me that fear had nothing to do with her unfulfilled desire to take up watercolor painting. She said, considering her workload, taking up painting was simply impossible. When I asked her what she did for a living, she told me she was a legal secretary and sold real estate on the side. Since I know each of these occupations alone can deliver sufficient means for most people to live on, I inquired further and asked her why she felt she needed to hold both jobs. Her answer: she was *afraid* she wouldn't have enough money in her old age. Before she could accept that fear was the source of her inability to paint, I had to remind her what she had just said. As long as she resisted acknowledging her fear, it kept protecting her belief about the lack of money and, in the process, blocking what she most desired.

Unconscious fear protects us from threats to our "self" (identity/existence) due to its involuntary relationship with emotions from which it draws its power.

Fear's Primary Function: The Self

Once I discovered the relationship between *unconscious* fear and my beliefs, I was awash in imponderable questions— the most pressing being, exactly what role do beliefs play in my life? Once I asked myself who am I? What distinguishes me as an individual, the answer emerged.

My immediate response to this question began with two words, "I am," after which followed several descriptive nouns: a wife, mother, artist, dog lover, etc. Exactly how I define my role as a wife almost certainly differs from yours. No matter. Everyone's beliefs differ, even in the same family. My sister never stopped trying to convince me that my experiences with Agnes never happened; they never happened to her, so they could not have happened to me.

Ultimately, *we are the sum of our beliefs,* known and unknown.

Fear equips each person with beliefs unique to them. As long as we are children, beliefs serve as positive influences. Because of them, we not only learn how to become a member of our families, but they give us the means to interact with one another as members of the human race. Because fear automatically preserves the inviolability of our childhood beliefs, they naturally follow us into adulthood.

As with clothes, we outgrow many beliefs that came in existence only to serve us as children. Unless fate has forced us to reevaluate them, chances are we are still relying on most of our childhood beliefs well past their "use-by" dates. In other words, past the period when we needed fear parenting us by protecting these beliefs, the fears supporting them, and, in the process, ostensibly preserving our existence and the sense of security we unconsciously derive from them. Most adult problems arise because we continue relying on these antiquated beliefs for security. Because of this, these dysfunctional beliefs become the source of conflict. Understanding the fundamental ways beliefs come into existence, as well as the different facets through which these unconscious beliefs impact our lives, can help us identify antiquated, dysfunctional beliefs that negatively impact our lives when the fears supporting them function operationally.

Basic Beliefs

I refer to the beliefs we acquire before puberty as our basic beliefs. These beliefs are the result of circumstances peculiar to our childhoods. Altogether, our basic beliefs form our primers for Life 101. These primers contain every belief we needed to safely maneuver through the labyrinth of early life. For example, when I was around five years old, against parental advice, I stuck my finger in a monkey's cage at a zoo. It bit me. The belief I took from this experience informed me to keep my fingers away from cuddly monkeys that happen to be alive. Unconsciously, I rely on the ways the fears supporting my basic beliefs work, as my psychological parents, to keep me behaving in ways that keep me safe. Thus, the beliefs in my primer were vital to surviving my childhood.

Basic beliefs materialize in two ways: actively conditioned beliefs and passively conditioned beliefs.

Actively Conditioned Beliefs

Actively conditioned beliefs are the result of things I was told as a child or events I experienced, such as the belief I adopted as a result of the monkey business just described.

Because my family repeatedly told me, "You are obnoxious," I adopted the belief that I was obnoxious, regardless of the validity of this opinion. Because recalling actively acquired or conditioned beliefs and their cause can be relatively easy, unearthing them and the reason for adopting them can be relatively straightforward.

The urge to conform, to fit in and belong, is a significant reason we adopt many beliefs. Thousands of years ago, if you couldn't conform, there was a real possibility you might be thrown out of the cave—and then where would you be? Fending for yourself? Surviving alone was not particularly desirable then, or for that matter, now. Thus, as if by osmosis, I slipped in as a member of my family by conforming. Unconsciously fearing rejection, I parroted my parents' opinions, attitudes, and beliefs; whatever my parents thought, I did too. Daddy's sisters were greedy; we were Episcopalians, Republicans, and disdained people who went on picnics. My mother thought my siblings hung the moon, especially my brother, being male and the presumed heir apparent. My sister was the perfect size, exactly like Mother. I was overweight, hysterical, and the bane of everyone's existence.

Passively Conditioned Beliefs

Then there are passively conditioned beliefs. They are the result of what *doesn't happen* to you. Due to their passive roots, unearthing these beliefs can be difficult. It took me years observing other mother-daughter relationships to realize how twisted mine was. Before then, I assumed all mothers were like mine and treated their daughters the way mine treated me. Knowing what I do now, I understand that my passively conditioned belief about mother/daughter relationships was a misconception. Knowing your family's history can help unearth some of these beliefs.

For instance, when my siblings were born, Mother and Daddy lived in a nondescript bungalow. Mother had nothing more pressing on her mind to attend to than her two children and husband. However, all that changed when my parents moved their family into the French provincial masterpiece Daddy had built. Coming from a relatively poor background, Mother was decidedly out of her element in what turned out to be an upper-class neighborhood. She had only Hollywood movies to inform her about her new life. Without help, her lack of sophistication could have had appalling results. I remember Mother once laughing about the star-studded décor she had once envisioned for her new living room. The architect recognized Mother's naiveté and put her in touch with a savvy interior decorator who convinced Mother the interior and exterior of a house such as hers should match. The result was truly exquisite.

Consequently, Mother became obsessed with being *the lady* of her refined new home. Once again, the only source Mother had to draw upon to show her how a lady should be and act were Hollywood movies. Her new identity began taking precedence over everything and everyone. Unfortunately, shortly after that, the unanticipated arrival of me spoiled that picture. From the time I was six months old, Mother hired someone to take care of me so she could preserve her new identity.

There was never a question Mother adored my siblings, but her adoration did not extend to me. After Agnes became my keeper, Mother's impenetrable apathy towards my plight sent an abundantly clear message: I didn't deserve better treatment. Something about me was decidedly wrong.

Due to their inscrutable origins, my passively conditioned beliefs remained deeply submerged. Some are still surfacing. In answer to the question, "Who am I?" I suspect none of these beliefs would have ever come to mind. In regards to the process of spiritual growth I am proposing, this is not a problem. Many beliefs may never surface which isn't a problem. Initiating spiritual growth requires unearthing only a small number of outgrown beliefs. Often this handful of beliefs will lead to the awareness of patterns of behavior, which in turn unearth knowledge of other beliefs.

A Summary of the Origins of Basic Beliefs

- A fear overwhelms an infant with emotion.

- Emotions threaten the child's ability to survive.

- The brain removes the threat by isolating the child's brain from awareness of fear and the emotions it is generating.

- Isolation creates a vacuum.

- The brain fills the vacuum with a reason that accounts for the presence of fear. When I learn language, I will come to recognize these reasons as beliefs.

- The reasons my childhood brain produces that turn into beliefs are based *on my current interpretation* of a situation.

- The behaviors that beliefs produce, repeated over time, program me like a computer—garbage in, garbage out. Programming relieves the brain from having to repeatedly reprocess fear.

- Thus, the goal of the original fear to protect my existence has been accomplished. My "self" as defined by my beliefs exists.

Guided by Beliefs

As a child, each belief saved my life in one way or another, no matter how distorted it was.

For a short time after Agnes started using me to maintain her sanity, I tried defending myself. Sad to say any effort I made was doomed, especially considering I was barely six years old when it all started. The thirty-year age difference aside, her gaslighting condemnations were so absurd, so ridiculously asinine, they defied rationality. But who was I to challenge my superior's accusations? No child has the confidence to do so. I was not only incapable of standing up for myself, but given Mother's passive attitude, it was obvious she had no intention to protect me. I simply acquiesced. Without alternate input, I was left to conclude I was unworthy of protection. I was a doormat.

My plight made sense as long as my behavior aligned with this belief. It gave me a role to play in the family scenario. Despite its implications, the belief gave me a much-needed sense of security. It accounted for the inexplicable aspects of my life and determined my attitudes and behaviors, reinforcing the belief. In this way, my life became a self-fulfilling prophecy.

I was astounded when I finally realized the extent of the damage that the behaviors this belief had been fomenting. For these reasons, the doormat's effects endured much longer and, therefore, have had a more significant impact throughout most of my life.

Security by Way of Preservation

Every belief your brain generates constitutes your reality. To preserve the integrity of this reality, operational fear rejects any idea, person or thing you do not already know. Anomalies, therefore, automatically register as threats in your brain. If you have never met an Inuit person growing up, should an Inuit family move in next door, you will likely be prejudiced against your new neighbors. The source of this prejudice is the unconscious need to preserve your sense of security. The upshot of this contrivance gives rise to such tragedies as racial discrimination.

Problems with accepting unknown, different things can be surprising. Shortly after Ken and I married, I made a fancy crab casserole as a celebratory gesture. My son Jack had never eaten crabmeat before. He insisted he couldn't eat the casserole because he claimed he could see the crab's beady little eyes looking up at him. Our policy was that he had to eat a "no-thank-you helping" (about one tablespoon full) to leave the table. After at least an hour of patiently waiting, Jack finally ate his "no-thank-you helping" and, of all things, asked for more. The foreign nature of the food threatened Jack's sense of security.

The phenomenon of like-minded human beings clumping together as a matter of security seems innocent enough. While being with people like us makes it easier for us to relate to each other, belonging to a particular group creates separation. The fact we are instinctively drawn to people like us is all well and good as long as we can also accommodate people who don't look like us, think like us, speak our language, have outlandish habits, wear peculiar clothes, or belong to the same club that we do. Unfortunately, because fear underlies human nature, unconscious beliefs force us to consider differences as threats.

When faced with diversity, fear goes into its protective mode. Regardless of the security this protection affords us, differences give rise to humanity's ugliest conflicts. Our history is replete with wars and the inconceivable amount of suffering they cause— unconsciously generated for the purpose of preserving someone's childhood belief and the security those beliefs allow so we can belong to the "right" group.

Thoughts to Ponder

♦ What were you repeatedly told as a child that is still affecting you?

♦ What beliefs form your identity?

♦ When faced with a peculiar new food, how do you react?

♦ Consider any racial prejudices you may have come across. What insecurities do they invoke?

♦ How often do these insecurities involve money?

♦ How does the idea of belonging affect your thoughts and behaviors?

Chapter 8

_____

Operational Fear

Fear ensures our survival through its unconscious, operational form commonly recognized as resistance. Resistance protects the "who" that is you from the "what" that is the death of your belief/body. The "how" is where problems arise. As it is the foundation of our beliefs, fear imposes strict limitations on what we believe. A perceived threat to a basic belief prompts unconscious fear to turn operational. Immediately, we experience resistance as a form of protection.

The following flow chart summarizes the operational ways in which fear functions.

Fear > Resistance > Emotions > Reactions > Conflict

- A perceived threat to a belief alerts fear.

- **Fear** unconsciously provokes resistance.

- **Resistance** triggers emotions.

- **Emotion** generates a reaction.

- The **Reaction**, or behavior, that resistance produces is specific to the belief it is protecting. For example, a cat scratches me, I respond with fear. This prompts me to believe cats are harmful and I hate cats; therefore, whenever I see a cat I react by running away.

- As a result, this unconsciously provoked reaction avoids the extinction of the belief that I hate cats and the harm they can inflict. This reaction protects the sanctity of the belief that my brain generated.

- Reactions are frequently disturbing, often precipitating **Conflicts** (later referred to as wolves).

Emotions

There are emotions and then there are feelings. We tend to lump both together and label them emotions. For my purposes, I make a distinction between emotions and feelings. According to Webster's definition, "emotion is a psychic and physical reaction (my emphasis)…that prepare(s) the body for immediate vigorous action." [6] While fear is an emotion, its reactions can appear as both positive and negative responses.

While we *feel* joy, bliss, and awe and label them emotions, because their source is the heart, not the brain, they are expressions of spirit. As an example of this distinction, in my early teenage years during the darkest period of Agnes' attacks on me, at the end of a midnight Christmas Eve service when the organist began playing "Hark! The Herald Angels Sing," inexplicable joy burst from my heart. Nothing in my life could account for this immense feeling of joy. Only spirit can inspire experiences like this. Fear generates emotions, emotions produce reactions. We express expressions of spirit as feelings.

Resistance draws its power from its ability to affect us emotionally. Its ability to incite emotions that cause us to react allowing fear, by way of resistance, to prevent our childhood beliefs from changing. According to this plan, changing a belief is the ultimate threat to our physical existence. Therefore, behind every emotion is an unconscious belief that you may or may not be aware exists. You feel happy because your expectation (belief) that your dog walker would show up on time happened; you are irritable because your furnace, which you may or may not realize you believe should keep going no matter what, stopped working. The unconscious protection we derive from resistance affords us a sense of security.

Emotions in particular, but resistance as well as reactions stand out as telltale signs of operational fear. The greater my familiarity with how these aspects register in my body, the faster I am able to grow spiritually.

Because the doormat developed as a way to protect me, the fear supporting the belief kept generating resistance to prevent me from acting any way contrary to that belief—the idea of entitlement would never have occurred to me. These unconscious prompts happened so automatically they *programmed my behavior.* This programming, therefore, worked to preserve the integrity of my belief. Due to resistance, childhood beliefs automatically follow you into adulthood. My family's prejudice was still part of my identity as an adult on the day of my Pivotal Event.

The purpose of resistance is to save our beliefs/selves from change or extinction; therefore, the emotional content of the reactions it generates will appear *highly disguised.* For this reason, identifying the emotions giving rise to a reaction can be exceedingly tricky. Mother had a "thing" about fat people. Fat was her barometer of acceptability. While her statements about fat people were always derisive, I never would have guessed they were emotionally driven before writing this book. And, too, I suspect Mother would have emphatically denied emotions had anything to do with her contempt of fat people. However, if the question was, "Do fat people repulse you?" there's no question Mother would have replied in the affirmative.

Resistance in Action

When we perceive a threat to our fear-based definition of our "self"/beliefs/existence, how fear causes us to react as adults may not always be in our best interests. For example, repeated rejection as a child made me afraid of further rejection. For years, resistance caused me to unconsciously push people away from me. The unconscious fear of rejection caused this reaction. While the behavior supported the belief, its reaction worked against what I deeply desired as an adult—to connect with people. Without my conscious interference, my life would not have changed.

Conflict often is the consequence of acquiescing to emotional charges. Conflicts can appear within yourself as stress, high blood pressure, or problems with other people. The emotional charge resistance discharged during my Pivotal Event unnerved me to the extent I reacted by refusing to attend the family meeting. As a child, having unconsciously adopted Mother's belief that her sisters-in-law were greedy to give me a sense of belonging, I had long outgrown needing the security that belonging to my family had given me. Nevertheless, because it functions unconsciously, resistance caused me to hold onto the prejudice long past its "use-by" date. Conflict ensued. The prospect of attending the reading of my aunt's will resurrected the family prejudice. Reacting to the emotional jolt from resistance, I conjured up a reason to stay home. This justification not only avoided the untimely death of my "self," it allowed my behavior to remain in compliance with my belief (prejudice).

Unfortunately, or fortunately as it were, the reaction didn't eliminate the inner conflict resistance had begun generating. Salvation came when I finally realized the reason I was resisting. Awareness allowed me to challenge the prejudice. Thus, I began emotionally healing myself.

The Reaction of Denial

Avoiding detection is paramount to how resistance functions since protecting our existence is the goal. Therefore, the intention of all the emotions and reactions that resistance manifests are meant to throw us off the scent.

Denial is the most obvious reaction that indicates resistance and, therefore, operational fear. Denials often appear camouflaged in forms of *blame, rationalization,* or *justification.*

The ability to deny responsibility may have originated to help children avoid being accountable for something they are ill-equipped to handle. Most lack the level of self-esteem to shoulder responsibility for their missteps. Raw vulnerability makes a child's developing sense of "self" susceptible to damage. The ability to deny protects a child's sense of security and shelters a child's feeling of being valued, both necessary for developing healthy egos.

Until we are old enough to take the blame for our actions and protect and defend ourselves, the ability to deny culpability is a positive reaction. When I was about five years old, I clearly remember choosing to lie rather than admit I was the one who ate the last Christmas cookie. Had I told the truth, my sister would have thrown me out of a game we were playing. For the sake of self-preservation, I denied I was the culprit. Denial saved me from being an outcast. When used by adults, though, the forms of denial indicate emotional immaturity.

The fact that expressions of denial appear in the Bible, many people assume these responses are acceptable. However, psychologically they are not healthy, especially when used by adults to avoid taking responsibility for their actions. The idea that "everyone does it" allows people to staunchly refuse to accept responses involving blame to be dysfunctional. For this reason, resistance poses the greatest obstacle to emotional and, spiritual growth.

Resistance can camouflage reactions so skillfully that they appear totally logical. All denials are not suspect, but most are or should be. During my Jungian studies, class discussions were most revealing when our group began the section on projection (the process of attributing a characteristic a person deems unacceptable to another person or thing). While spotting other people's projections was never a problem, no one could recognize their own, including me. Once, when one of my classmates dared to point out I was projecting, I immediately reacted by denying it. Resistance generated this reaction to prevent me from recognizing the belief I was defending. I had probably outgrown the belief, but because my psychological parent (the operational function of unconscious fear) equated it with my existence, it was not in my best interest to question the belief. Now, I understand reactions like this are red flags that indicate resistance.

Even though denials squelch ownership of reactions that might call attention to its presence, these attempts to are only temporary. They are never a solution. Resistance will keep levying denials until the outgrown belief generating it causes so much disruption if forces us to address and transform it. Not addressing the root of a conflict and avoiding ownership of it leads to a life of discord and suffering, much of which defines the human condition.

Denial, in whatever form it takes, foments problems that can be highly dangerous. As a new mother in 1966, my choice to nurse my son, Jack, ran against the popular trend of bottle-feeding. I would have sworn my choice to nurse Jack was a conscious decision. In truth, it wasn't. If there was ever a time my mother glowed, it was as she recounted nursing the three of us. There was no question that breastfeeding ranked high on Mother's list of approved behaviors. Without knowing it, by choosing to nurse Jack, I was seeking the "brownie points" from Mother that I'd never earned before. However, after my second son was born, the same impulse that had functioned positively with Jack set off a sequence of detrimental events with the new baby, Edward. My extensive rationalizations brought both Edward and me within a hair's breadth of death.

I brought Edward home from the hospital with a bladder infection and enough antibiotics to eliminate it. Several days later, though, I started getting chills and fever indicative of childbed fever, a life-threatening disease in postpartum women. The additional infection proved to be more than the antibiotics could handle. Nevertheless, I steadfastly kept the extent of my illnesses a secret. In the back of my mind, I feared exposing the truth would curtail nursing, which meant an end to the brownie points. To make matters worse, during this period, a wrinkled, gray area appeared on my left breast that indicated a breast infection. All the material I'd read about breastfeeding warned against continuing to nurse with an infection of this sort, but was I going to call attention to this, either? Sure that if I called my doctor, he would insist I stop nursing, or worse, hospitalize me, especially in light of my childbed fever, I rationalized doing nothing once again. The worst was yet to come. One morning when I went to nurse Edward, I observed a gray cast to his body. Again, I chose to ignore it. I was sure the domino effect of taking Edward to the doctor would undoubtedly end breastfeeding. How and why we both survived I don't know. It certainly wasn't because I was a conscientious mother—far from it. In the face of my elaborate, convoluted justifications, an objective, rational decision was beyond impossible.

Frozen

The types of conflicts that resistance foments are legion and rarely identifiable. No matter how innocuous its presentation, the source of a conflict always needs to be investigated. The flawed sense of security that beliefs offer leads people to resolutely resist change. Clinging to our beliefs rather than facing the unknown that change portends can be disastrous. At the end of her life, based on her feeble attempts to reach out to me after my sister died, I suspect Mother wanted to change, but that proved impossible. Her negative opinion of me had been ingrained for so long that it immobilized her. You may remember that the pit of hell in Dante's *Inferno* was frozen. This certainly was the case with Mother. Even though she was still physically alive, she became a member of the living dead, as defined by her seeming lack of growth.

Due to resistance, the script of beliefs that some of us fashion in childhood never changes. For those of us in this situation, our life remains frozen. Our outgrown scripts have little to do with our current circumstances, but change? Never. Flannery O'Connor summed up this problem in her short story, "A Good Man is Hard to Find," with the Misfit's comment about an uppity old grandmother. [7] "She would have been a good woman," the Misfit said, "if it had been somebody there to shoot her every minute of her life." The grandmother had preserved her script of beliefs long past the time she needed their protection. For this reason, all her life they had been working against her, making her someone no one enjoyed having around. When the Misfit puts a gun to her head, it forces the woman to finally break out of her script and become the woman her script had been squelching.

If somebody had been there to shoot Mother every minute of her life, she too might have been able to shed the straightjacket her childhood beliefs bound her in, limiting her ability to express love. Letting people touch her heart might have turned her into a compassionate, caring person, as opposed to the cold-hearted woman she presented to those around her.

At the end of her days, Agnes' life-long reliance on denial tragically caught up with her. Sometime during my forties, a situation arose that necessitated I consult a psychiatrist. Unfortunately, the only one I knew was the man who never believed what I'd had told him about my past was true, but I was desperate. During the appointment, the subject of how Agnes treated me came up. I confessed how much I had longed to ask her why she had been so cruel. After all, when she took charge, I was only a small child, one who just wanted to be loved as Nettie had loved me. Having said this, the doctor suggested he and I go together to question Agnes, who was living in a retirement home. Even if the question of my welfare was the reason he suggested the visit, I strongly suspect, on some level, that the man really wanted to find out if the stories I'd told him were true. Before we went, he had me arm him with as many memories about interactions with Agnes as I could recall.

On the day of the visit, I asked Agnes a big question, "How could you have been so cruel to me? I was just a child who wanted to be loved."

Her response was natural, but so unexpected it shocked me speechless. She denied everything. Agnes insisted nothing extraordinary had ever happened between us.

The conversation would have ended at this point had I interrogated her on my own. The fact that I had armed my doctor with my memories allowed him to take over and ask her about specific incidents. Being challenged by a man, not just any man, but one of authority, his confrontation stripped Agnes of all pretensions. When he brought up the knife incident, Agnes had to concede it was true; I had held a knife above her head once. However, having admitted this, she airily dismissed the entire incident, saying, "It was nothing, totally unimportant."

The psychological safe house of denial had been Agnes' refuge for forty years. The role she had worked so hard to create and preserve, her existence as the treasured housekeeper, as Mother was so fond of portraying her to anyone willing to listen, depended on denial. But those halcyon days were long gone. I suspect Agnes could not admit, even to herself, that she could be guilty of any wrongdoing. Still so deeply entrenched in her hallowed identity, coming face to face with the reprehensible, vile behavior that had caused me to take such a reprehensible action was too appalling for her to accept.

On an unconscious level, her identity crashed headlong into the truth. The collision detonated more psychological wreckage than the poor woman could handle. *On that day,* Agnes stopped eating. Two weeks later, almost to the exact hour of our last exchange, Agnes died. Did I feel responsible for her death? Initially I did, but that quickly passed when I realized that her inability to accept the truth about herself had been so horrific she couldn't handle it.

Fear will always be part of our lives, mainly by way of our beliefs, as it offers several benefits. The most important of which is a universally agreed-upon reality. Beliefs people the world over share, such as the sky is blue, or snow is cold, create a collective perception. The universality of this perception allows humans worldwide to interact and bond with each other. Like knowing that I get sick when I eat too much of my favorite chocolate, the results of giving the beliefs operational fear supports free reign can be disastrous.

Thoughts to Ponder

♦ What actions might you be currently justifying or rationalizing?

♦ Consider taking responsibility, if only to yourself, for behavior you've been justifying. How does that feel?

♦ Think about a recent conflict. Consider what belief might be its source.

♦ If you dare, ask someone close to you to tell you about the frozen parts of your life they've observed. We all have them to some degree.

Chapter 9

Your Worst Enemy
Yourself

We, like the characters in the film *The Truman Show,* follow a script. Our scripts are the basic beliefs that comprise our primers for Life 101. The goal of our psychological parents, as well as that of the directors of *The Truman Show,* is to ensure their subjects adhere to their script. Towards this end, both our psychological parents and the directors use fear to manipulate their subjects so that their subjects never stray from their scripts.

Due to resistance's unconscious promptings, we behave as if the script of our basic beliefs, identity (self), existence, and security are one and the same thing. To ensure the infallibility of this erroneous supposition, resistance causes us to reject outright anything contrary to our script. We reject anything *different:* any thought, idea, or type of person who does not act according to our scripts or look like us, as a matter of self-preservation. Theoretically, we feel safe if our present life mirrors our past. In this way, fear continually works to keep the security blanket of our scripts mended and spotless. Had I gone off script as a child and expected to be treated as anything other than an unlovable doormat, aberrant behavior would have brought further emotional injury upon myself.

As an adult, when something I am involved in resonates with a past event that had elicited a fear experienced in childhood, operational fear immediately incites resistance; the unconscious assumption is that my life might be in jeopardy. This assumption instigated my Pivotal Event. By causing me to avoid attending the family meeting operational fear "saved" my life represented by the untimely death of the prejudice that had allowed me to believe I was not greedy. The chain of behaviors operational fear generated allowed this belief to remain in compliance with my script.

Garbage In, Garbage Out

Our brains, like computers, program our behaviors so that our psychological parents can avoid having to constantly reprocess basic fears. Programmed behaviors allow a smoother pathway through life, affording us a much-needed source of security.

During my childhood I avoided Agnes by going on walks in the woods or playing in the attic. As a result, I was programed to seek isolation. As I grew into adulthood, though, this behavior began manifesting conflicts out of the wazoo. Problems arose when I went to college. I found I wanted to be involved with people, to belong, to be included, and to have friends. Truth be told, I didn't just want to belong; I was *desperate* to belong. I longed to be considered an acceptable person—an affirmation I imagined belonging would give me. Sure, as a teenager I had had acquaintances galore, but no real friends, the kind to whom you entrust your most intimate thoughts. My programming made friendships close to impossible.

My grievous relationships with females amplified the problem. I had no idea how to act with other women.

Desperate to connect, unconsciously, I broadcasted a wanton neediness that put people off. No matter how much I wanted to change, my programming kept my ability to connect with other women in irons. Then, when nothing else worked, I got the bright idea (which was an offshoot of my programming, but I didn't know it at the time) of becoming a "pleaser." I decided placing others' needs before mine would buy me friends, and it did. Only, the women my "pleaser" attracted were, with very few exceptions—clones of Agnes, attracted by the power my suppliant behavior gave them.

It's hard to imagine anyone wanting to be abused, but abuse is precisely what I unconsciously sought. It was what I knew. The familiarity of abusive situations, as warped as they were, made me feel secure despite the pain they invariably caused. Anyone, or any problem, that was not abusive had to be shaped up or discarded. My mind treated the foreign nature of acceptance as a threat. Freshman year in college, a truly good and loving man fell in love with me, really loved me. When the extent of his adoration finally dawned, I became desperate to escape. To make matters worse, there was no earthly reason to reject the guy. He was a beautiful human being, a seminary student studying to become an Episcopal priest, but reject him I did.

At that time, the Universe could have thrown a legion of Prince Charmings at my feet—maybe a chance encounter at a bookstore with Johnny Depp or Harrison Ford, during which they would fall madly in love with me. Tough luck, boys. My doormat's approved list of experiences didn't include hunks the likes of you falling for the likes of me.

The doormat spawned related beliefs like the notion I couldn't defend myself. One time an irate college professor accused me of something my friend did, but never admitted. It took me years to realize why this friend insisted on treating me to dinner that night after this incident. All I wanted to do was to go back to my dorm room and crawl under my bed. Since I had accepted the rap for what my friend had done, she needed a way to thank me. And so, this was how my life continued for thirty more years.

After I married Ken, the wolves my programming generated expanded exponentially. Unbeknownst to either of us, Ken was unconsciously programmed to serve his clients first; me and the children's needs came second, always. In retrospect, I am sure the marriage wouldn't have lasted a year without my doormat directing calling the moves. During the two months of our courtship, we saw each other just about every day. The week after we married, for great swaths of time, Ken came home only to sleep. Any confrontation I needed to initiate about these outrageous absences had to happen in the middle of the night. But how could I, a doormat, be so intrusive as to awaken him for something I needed? The massive shame I assumed as a doormat paralyzed me. Only when living in a phantom of marriage became so unbearable that anguish finally shattered my paralysis was I able to confront him.

Ken would always promise to do better. Next Saturday, he'd proclaim, he would stay home all day. That Friday night I would happily drift off to sleep in anticipation of our day together. When Saturday dawned, he'd finally confess, darn it, he had to go to the office after all, but, and this statement was always the clincher, just for a couple of hours. Only, those couple of hours somehow always managed to miraculously lengthen and take up the entire day. Having already behaved contrary to my programming to confront him in the first place, I was all too willing to go along with whatever excuses he gave. I kept justifying his failures until desperation would once again reach an explosive level. Nothing changed. No matter how often I promised myself I would insist he keep his word, I always acquiesced. Like a helicopter mother, my programming was always there to remind me that— Mother always knows best for you, dear.

Protection Gone Awry

As I grew older, maintaining my programming as a pleaser generated unrelenting conflict. The decision to finally do something about that pebble in my shoe required reaching a level of distress so painful I couldn't endure its presence another day. But leave the security of my comfy hiding place and choose to change without reaching a level of discomfort? You've got to be kidding! Unless you have pursued emotional growth on your own, in all probability, resistance is still micromanaging your life as it did mine, and to some extent, it still does. Based on how I behave, if fear had a body and could voice an opinion, it would claim I am still a child. Even though infants have no choice but to allow fear to micromanage their lives, nothing requires an adult to continue being micromanaged.

During my years as Agnes' captive, I probably would have gone insane had I not begun expressing on paper the anger I was not entitled to express otherwise. I must have written reams of pages that always started with, "Dearest best friend of my enemy." The significance of this address did not occur to me at the time. It was just a way to begin releasing the malicious stink of ugliness slathered upon me that day. In retrospect, the implication is clear. The attachment to my script prevented me from taking the necessary steps to help myself, and so I became my own worst enemy.

This is precisely the root of the behavioral problem many adults experience.

Imbued With Idiosyncratic Powers

Woe be to anyone who dares tamper with an obsolete cultural belief!

Any attempt to rip away one of these precious blankies that resistance has scrupulously protected for decades is doomed. The actions people take to preserve their hallowed beliefs can be as incredible as the steps some women take to avoid the bodily changes that naturally come with age. On some level we might realize accepting new ideas might be helpful, but no. Our unconscious attachments to the beliefs from which we derive our sense of security close our minds. During the days when Covid-19 was causing a global pandemic, even in the face of danger, many people in the United States still demanded everyone return to their old routines. As we now know, keeping to those routines during the early days of the pandemic put lives at risk, but the security that our programming unconsciously promised overruled logic.

Once an antiquated creed is labeled "traditional," robotic repetition gives it unwarranted inviolability, whether scientific or religious. The stamp of "traditional" reinforces a false sense of security that swindles people into crediting these beliefs with peculiar powers that release believers from ever needing to question these beliefs. Traditional tales become accepted as fact: *a snake* convinced Eve to eat the forbidden fruit—really? Beliefs with all the solidity of my granddaddy's conviction about the sin of eating meat on Friday keep such beliefs afloat regardless of the suffering they foment. To be sure, Granddaddy had the authority of *the Church* supporting his conviction, but, er, as things turned out, the Church *changed its mind*—actually changed its mind about what *they alleged* was a *sin?* Wow. Writ in stone now and forever, once a sin, always a sin—I guess not.

Swindled by Beliefs

The assumption about the indisputable nature of sin, or any belief, is merely another example of "The Emperor's New Clothes." According to the folktale, swindlers were trying to sell the emperor what they claimed was a special cloth. If someone couldn't see the material, it was because they were unfit for their job or were exceptionally stupid. Rooted in and perpetuated by fear, the swindlers' story and clothes were an ingeniously fabricated illusion. Of course, the emperor could not admit that he was unable to see the cloth. So, he bought it. When he started parading around the village, showing off his new clothes, it was obvious the new clothes did not exist. Fearing what would happen if they exposed the truth, the villagers eagerly followed the swindlers' story. No one dared speak up, but what happened when an innocent child told the emperor he had no clothes on? The charade collapsed.

Never assume beliefs or behaviors are healthy, or for that matter, accurate even though everyone you know believes the same thing or behaves the same way. If a sin is not always a sin, might not all dogmas be like the emperor's new clothes—as ephemeral and as transient as every belief the human mind has birthed? Each time we avoid questioning a belief, regardless of its source, we shore up its power and strengthen our attachment to it. The nature of any belief, religious or not, should always be subject to questioning.

Due to the way resistance swindles us into defending the illusion our childhood beliefs establish, it affects traditional beliefs the same way. As a result, these beliefs become immortalized; therefore, suffering remains the status quo.

Apron-String Attachments

The idiom "apron strings" has been bandied about for so long that it might not be clear it refers to the emotional bond between children and their parents. The work of resistance is to make us so attached to our basic beliefs that unconsciously we equate our *beliefs* with being our *lives,* our very existence. Therefore, we treat them as our life preservers based on the unconscious assumption that without our beliefs there is no "self," we do not exist. The absurdity of this supposition cannot be denied. Regardless, resistance guards the integrity of this supposition with the ferocity of a mother elephant so that no matter what, under threat, resistance will interject emotions and reactions on our behalf. As a result, we become emotionally attached to our beliefs—developing apron-string attachments to them just like people sometimes do with their parents.

The older we are, the greater the likelihood we have numerous outgrown childhood beliefs that need updating. Even though resistance may be making life miserable, the tendency is to stay the course as designed by our scripts—which happens to be the very effect unconscious fear works to produce. And so, we snuggle deeper into our blankies—our fear-based security systems—and defend our beliefs. We resist change at all costs, sometimes to the death. Resistance can inspire irrational, extreme behaviors—nominally "pro-life" antiabortionists *willing to kill* doctors they suspect of performing abortions.

Here's the question. Is this boxed-in, limited life the kind of existence you really want to perpetuate?

One Christmas, my brother received a tape recorder. After he captured my sister exclaiming on tape, "I found a price tag!" he spliced it together so her comment was continuously repeated. Hearing this inane comment repeatedly became so irritating that the whole family was ready to throttle him. Programming affects us in much the same way. We become our worst enemy when we ignore outdated beliefs. The programming from outdated beliefs can make us feel like we are hamsters running on a wheel. No matter how hard we run we never get anywhere because programming creates self-fulfilling prophecies—once a doormat, always a doormat.

Apron-string attachments to these parents are detrimental to emotional and, therefore, spiritual growth. On the surface, emotional and spiritual growth seem mutually exclusive. However, the spiritual growth I am proposing requires putting our psychological parents out of commission. The first and only requirement for this form of growth is emotional growth. Facing the fears involved in emotional growth is a challenge in itself, but the sense of security that fear unconsciously promises compounds the problem. Emotional growth can erase those issues.

Moving from Kentucky to Minnesota was the best thing that has happened to me. No one here (except for my sons and their families) knew the first thing about the old me. The box of beliefs that my upbringing imposed on me mainly stayed in Kentucky. It wasn't until we moved that I clearly realized that the contents of that box were the beliefs my family needed to believe about me in order to justify the way they were abusing me. Those beliefs reflected nothing about the human being I am.

As long as we remain ignorant of the way unconscious factors block our ability to grow spiritually, we allow our psychological parents to continue throwing us off track.

Thoughts to Ponder

♦ Are some of the difficult incidents from your past still affecting you today? How?

♦ What belief might be your own worst enemy?

♦ Routines aside, if your life seems like you are running on a hamster wheel, does the idea of change feel threatening? If so, why?

Chapter 10

Bottom Line

Security

F ear exists only in our physical reality; therefore, everything fear supports, including our sense of security, lacks permanence.

Change is the only constant in life. Death is a given. The last thing the physical world can guarantee is freedom from loss. When a tornado blew through Louisville, Kentucky in 1974, it destroyed a man's highly insured stand of one-hundred-year-old oak trees. Insured or not, replacing these majestic trees precisely as they were before the storm was impossible. The transplants had to be much younger, smaller trees. They were no match for the magnificent trees the tornado uprooted. No amount of prestige, insurance, or wealth can prevent loss, despite the current notion of security that implies freedom from concerns involving loss.

If the choice had been left up to us, would we have knowingly consigned our sense of security to our beliefs? I doubt it. Like most people, my source of security was the reality as defined by my beliefs. However, continued reliance on this form of security can be disastrous.

The foundation of this security is the fallacious assumption that fear unconsciously supports, that beliefs and existence are the same thing [have belief; cannot die].

As a consequence, championing personal beliefs can quickly turn destructive. As captives of their beliefs, we see "Christian" parents disowning their LGBTQ+ children, and pro-lifers ironically killing doctors who perform abortions. Heinous acts committed by human beings—all done to defend truths unconsciously associated with personal security.

Dissatisfaction and suffering will rule the day as long as human beings remain enslaved by their unconscious fears. Due to conflict, suffering will continue unabated as long as we remain loyal to the vacuous form of security that our basic beliefs promise. In the Western world, bodies are healthier and live longer, but to what end? To suffer one more day? Without achieving the steadfast form of security that spiritual growth offers, the same behaviors that have been causing suffering throughout our history will continue. Again and again, and once again, the refrain continues echoing, "Will we ever learn?" This ceaseless recycling of issues occurs both personally and globally. Just this morning on the radio, there was a report that a politician is raising the issue of putting a copy of the Ten Commandments in every public schoolroom. *Again?*

Never Enough

Without a fulfilling spiritual life, starvation lurks behind every achievement and every paycheck. There can never be enough as long as fear is able to micromanage our thoughts unconsciously. Due to the transient nature of beliefs, dependence on them (and the fear that supports them) for security leaves a vacuum of meaning; the abyss of never having enough. This sense of emptiness forces some people to keep hoovering up more wealth than they could ever need or use. An acquaintance of mine, whose husband is a highly successful surgeon, once complained that every time her husband reached one of his goals, and she began to think at long last they could relax, he would come up with another more significant, more wonderful something he must achieve. Winning the lottery might temporarily satisfy a thirst for security, or a person might attract Mr. or Ms. Perfect, but after the Rolex, the yacht, the Learjet, and houses in all the right places, how much more does it take to satisfy the need for security? Advertisements in upscale media, such as the glossy monthly *WSJ Magazine,* a publication of the *Wall Street Journal,* attest to the pathetic, over-the-top substitutes available for those who can afford them—millions spent for the sole purpose of eliminating that indefinable sense of emptiness.

The conventional assumption is that more money will finally bring happiness, success, or whatever, but it never does. That desirable something out there will always exist just beyond reach. Because it is an illusion, material security can evaporate in an instant: stock markets crash, pandemics arise, wildfires destroy homelands, wars displace hundreds of thousands of people, and so on.

Years ago, National Public Radio reported a survey they conducted of people at all income levels. [8] The point of the survey was to discover if people were ever satisfied with the amount of money they were making. The reporter asked each interviewee to state how much money they were already being paid and how much more it would take to feel they had enough.

Across the board, from the family making less than $50,000 to the one making over $1.5 million a year, each respondent was sure that if they could only make just X amount more, they would finally feel they had enough.

The lack of satisfaction in these responses illustrates the abyss of never having enough. As long as the physical, fear-based world defines security, the idea of a sustained sense of fulfillment will remain the stuff of dreams.

Without spiritual sustenance, human beings will remain hostages to their Sisyphean plights, endeavoring to achieve that ineffable something just beyond reach. Thus, the corrosive recycling of conflict and suffering plaguing humanity since the beginning of time will continue.

Genuine Security

The only permanent source of security is spirit. The form of emotional growth I am proposing switches a person's source of security from the physical to the spiritual body. Founded in spirit's timeless wellspring of love, this form of security is eternal, indestructible and not subject to change or loss. If we could only access our spiritual essence in our youth when our brains are pliable, open enough to begin forming a relationship with spirit, its security could eliminate so much suffering later in life. The ability to access my spirit not only helps me make the choices that determine the quality of my day, but it also serves as a permanent source of security.

The more I can rely on my spiritual connection for direction and security, the easier it is to surf the chaos the physical world whips up. The distracting things people do and say that formerly threw me off-balance rarely faze me now. The way I react now when dealing with a hostile situation, sometimes heals and unites people. In the past my reactions often added to a problem.

Spiritual security creates trust in myself. Consequently, I am slowly realizing my potential as a human being.

Hold Your Nose and Jump

Most of us have everything we need to heal ourselves. Determination and courage are the most critical requirements for stepping out of our comfort zones to make the choice to change. Ken unexpectedly died two days before Christmas. As you might imagine, this sudden loss of my partner of close to forty-nine years put me in a tailspin. Initially, my focus had to be settling Ken's will as best as possible, which was sometimes questionable. Self-soothing behaviors like working jigsaw puzzles and reading filled my time. When faced with an unfamiliar activity, I felt like I was facing a wall. It became apparent something had to change; I had to force myself to get off my behind. The painting I began just before Ken died kept niggling at me. Finally, some four months after his death, I told myself I had to work on it for a minimum of fifteen minutes, which magically turned into several hours with questionable results, to be sure. At least, working on the painting gave me a way to go through the wall.

Choosing to change a belief might make you feel anxious, like jumping off a cliff. Just remember, this sense of intimidation is how operational fear keeps you safe. This is understandable, knowing how long we have been unconsciously associating our beliefs with our existence. Can beliefs prevent death? Of course not, that is up to our bodies and fate. Because it involves transforming childhood beliefs that we identify as representing our "selves," our identities, changing a belief could be considered a form of dying to the "self."

The choice is simple. Think about the miserable life people suffer when they remain vassals to their unconscious fears like my former caregiver, Agnes. If they could only realize the benefits, I think most people would prefer the challenge of emotional/spiritual growth rather than continuing to run on their hamster wheels.

Thoughts to Ponder

♦ What do you rely on for security?

♦ If you take a particular route to work daily, try a different route. How does this small change make you feel, especially about making other changes?

Part III

The Exercises

Chapter 11

Peas to Pearls

Two Exercises for Spiritual Liberation

The focus of the two exercises in this chapter is the emotional growth required for the type of spiritual growth I am proposing. Emotional growth resolves conflicts and unclogs our brains, which frees our hearts to grow spiritually. There exist numerous ways to grow emotionally, but not many actually change the way a person behaves as these exercises can.

Numerous beliefs whose behaviors befitted our needs as children no longer do in adulthood. Circumstances change, but unfortunately, our juvenile beliefs cannot change of their own volition. Often, adults unconsciously respond as they did as children due to the inability of beliefs to naturally evolve in keeping with our growing bodies. My father took a picture of me wearing a green dress the morning I entered first grade. If I could still wiggle into that dress it would look ridiculous on me now. Likewise, the beliefs that served as my safe house in childhood often are in conflict with my desires as an adult. The incontrovertible indicator of an outgrown belief is the conflict that its behavior generates.

As I mentioned earlier, because our childhood beliefs were conceived in fear, unconsciously, the fear is programmed to keep protecting our lives no matter what.

Detection is treated as a threat. What we most desire always appears camouflaged due to the mental gridlock that fear unconsciously causes.

In the fairy tale "The Princess and the Pea," the princess could always feel the pea hidden under her mattress regardless of how many more mattresses were piled on top of it. So it is with the conflicts that outgrown beliefs spawn. Personal conflicts, like the pea under the mattress, will keep making themselves known until we resolve them. Evasive measures can neither alter nor eliminate the problems they create. Resistance is always at the ready to ensure your basic beliefs never change so that, according to how operational fear works, you don't end up six feet under. Any attempt to change a problematic behavior without first addressing its belief and its underlying fear is a lost cause. Let's turn now to the two exercises that address beliefs, the first of which is Good Parenting.

Exercise #1: The Five Major Parts of Good Parenting

It is nearly impossible to change a dysfunctional behavior once established. The problems it generates will keep increasing until you are forced to grow up and, as an independent adult who can stand on their own, take charge of your life and start taking responsibility for your behavior—the result of good parenting. Until then, this psychological parent (the system through which operational fear manages your life) can't imagine you taking responsibility for yourself. According to this parent, premature exposure might be your undoing. While completing the following exercises, the slightest indication of indecision on your part will cause your psychological parent to resume control. Therefore, you must prove three things: 1) that you are *genuinely committed* to facing and accepting your childhood fears; 2) that you have the courage *to take responsibility* for your actions; and 3) that you are strong enough to *admit being wrong* and *defend* yourself. For this reason, independence is also the goal of this parent.

The first exercise, divided into five parts, addresses unconscious childhood fears. Delving into the unconscious might concern some people. The reports of early twentieth-century encounters with the unconscious have given it a bad reputation. The original investigators seem to have plunged into the vat of their unconscious without a clear intent. Understandably, for this reason, they were overwhelmed. The following exercise uses a focused, *noninvasive* method that addresses only a specific unconscious aspect. The intent of this focused approach produces positive results. The most sobering aspect you will encounter is compassion for your infantile self when you address a childhood fear.

While you cannot un-ring a bell, you can unravel an unconscious fear generating a detrimental belief. Your perspective is the most incisive tool at your disposal. The fear will never disappear completely; however, because it is no longer unconscious, awareness gives you the ability to control it and actually *change* the behavior that its belief supported. As you begin the exercise, the immature understanding that gave rise to the belief in question will become apparent.

Good Parenting Part I – Pinpointing the Obstacle

This first part of the Good Parenting exercise involves seven steps for you to complete.

Step 1. Focus on something you've longed to have or do. With your mind focused on this desire, ask yourself what you are feeling. Where or how is the feeling registering in your body? These sensations can appear in many ways: from twinges in your solar plexus, throat, and heart to hyperventilating, stiffness in the neck, sweaty palms, or even stuttering. Because you are unique, the fear of the sensations elicited will be unique to you. For example, I felt tightness in my throat whenever I staged another "pleaser" stunt. In retrospect, the feeling was eerily reminiscent of the way the chorus of three, meaning my mother, sister, and brother, kept trying to throttle me.

Step 2. Once you identify the physical sensation, amplify that feeling to its extreme.

Step 3. With the feeling heightened, ask yourself what this feeling might be expressing. Whatever thought comes to mind is articulating the unconscious fear preventing you from achieving the goal you focused on in Step 1. If the reason seems so logical and rational, you don't believe fear is involved—remember, operational fear, by way of resistance, has spent a lifetime working to keep you ignorant. Now is not the time to acquiesce and continue allowing it to keep your power under wraps.

The answer might not be immediately apparent. Identifying the fear may require approaching it from a different angle, perhaps discussing the thoughts that come to mind with another person. This is how the woman I mentioned in Chapter 7, who, having attended one of my workshops, finally discovered the fear that had convinced her she could not take up watercolor painting. Then there are times when I feel resistance, but pinpointing the fear sustaining it remains elusive. When this happens, employing one of the creative tools suggested below can help give it expression. Whichever of the following tools you choose, begin at Step 2 with the sensation heightened.

Writing about the fear using stream-of-consciousness journaling can be very helpful. As you begin, ask the fear what it wants you to know. Then, without thinking, let your words pour out of the tip of your pen. Write down any ideas that come to mind. Remember, you are writing for your eyes only. Just let the words flow without concern for spelling or grammar. If nothing comes to mind initially, try writing with your nondominant hand.

Another suggestion is draw or paint a picture with the emotion intensified. When I began investigating the beliefs surrounding Agnes' impact on me, resistance drowned out my ability to think. So, I resorted to drawing. With feelings intensified, I drew a picture of my first memory of Agnes and her mother. We had just picked them up at the train station and were on the drive home. The two foreigners sat side by side in the middle seat of Mother's station wagon, one of the first wood-trimmed wagons Ford produced that sported three rows of seats, while my friend and I sat behind them in the third seat. My drawing showed sparks emanating from all around the backs of these women. The picture I drew was right on target—sparks of anger emanating from around the two women.

Another helpful tool can be to dance with the intensified emotion or act it out. Your body holds the emotion. Any movement you feel comfortable doing will help loosen and free the emotion that will bring it to mind. If you are in a situation where none of these suggestions is feasible, have a conversation with the feeling as I once did while on vacation in the late '80s. I had spent the first part of the vacation developing my workshop on a psychological approach to spiritual growth. After completing the first section one evening, I promised to resume work first thing in the morning; however, when the next day dawned, instead of keeping my promise to myself from the night before, I allowed trivial things to sway me off track.

When lunchtime came, I found Ken sitting on the dock, just reading. I was furious. He should be *doing something*, I thought. But no there he was, simply sitting, doing nothing, just reading. Then, to make matters worse, after lunch I found him in the cottage lounging on the couch reading again! That did it. I pounced, "What on earth are you doing just sitting around reading all day? We're on vacation. *You need to be doing something*," I wailed. The poor man tried to defend himself. He even suggested that the problem might be mine. Ha! Not on your life! "I'm the responsible one in this family," I retorted. My state of irritation kept escalating as I continued ignoring the promise I had made to myself. By that evening, my ire had expanded to include our daughter, Maggie. As embarrassing as it is to admit this, after dinner, during a game of Scrabble, the thought actually occurred to me that Ken and Maggie were conspiring against me. That idea so unnerved me, I decided I had to go to bed. With trepidation, in the isolation of our bedroom, I risked recording the day's events in my journal. I was still so deeply entrenched in resistance that nothing substantial showed up, but the little that did was enough to allow me to fall asleep.

Still in the clutches of resistance, the following day I decided to go on the walk that Ken and I usually went on together, but alone. No doubt it came as a relief to Ken. After walking a mile or so without reprieve, the discomfort became intolerable. As much as laying the blame on Ken had been gratifying, in a mean sort of way, it resolved nothing. Blaming only magnified the problem. Stranded in the middle of the woods, I decided to dialogue with the feeling. The issue didn't take long to surface.

Ken had been right all along; the problem was mine. As a child, I had adopted my Germanic family's work ethic, which included many "shoulds." When I broke my promise to myself, resistance began unconsciously storming me with childhood shoulds. The storm increased each time I ignored a should's emotional "tell," elbowing into my brain.

Owning up to the truth to myself was difficult enough, but how could I face telling Ken about this fear I'd just unearthed? Alas, as life would have it, about this time, ol' Ken Tuggle appeared on the trail, walking in my direction. Part of me desperately wanted to save face and run away and keep blaming Ken for being the cause of my problem. However, if I continued feeding my self-righteous snit, which resistance was nurturing, the situation would only worsen. So, with eyes averted, I confessed all, expecting anger in return, but anger was the last thing on Ken's mind. He only wanted harmony, probably more than I did then (giving up a great snit can be really hard). But I needn't have worried, Ken was totally accepting. Immediately, he forgave me. The sudden release of all the conflict that resistance had been fomenting was cleansing beyond anything I could have imagined.

The final three steps of this first part of the Good Parenting exercise may seem odd, but please don't let that deter you. They are crucial.

Step 4. With the emotion intensified, conjure an image of a human figure that best embodies the character of the feeling being expressed. For example, the visual embodiment of the fear preventing the woman in my workshop from painting might be a shriveled-up, arthritic old hag.

Step 5. Now, give that person a name, one that is descriptive of the emotion or issue in question. If possible, make the name silly, but related to the problem. For example, a name for the arthritic old hag might be Minnie Miser. Whatever name you choose, make sure you don't already know someone by that name.

Step 6. Now ask that imaginary spokesperson the following questions:

- How have you been protecting me? From what or whom?

- What do you want me to know?

Step 7. Now, thank your fear for all the help it has given you and tell it you are ready to take control.

The answers that come to mind can be revealing. One of the first times I used these exercises to solve a problem, I had just been discovered as an artist by the owner of a Fifty-Seventh Street gallery in New York City. I'd hit the big time. At one point the gallery owner even expressed interest in representing me, even though she had only represented men in the past. This was jaw-droppingly amazing. Now, she was entertaining the idea of representing a woman—me! However, representation hung on one thing: the sale of the only pastel that was small enough to send to her gallery that was left over from the show she saw in Louisville. (The pastel hadn't sold in Louisville, so why would it sell in New York?) Nevertheless, even if the picture did sell, a more significant problem loomed.

The woman refused to show my present body of work as displayed in Louisville: pastels the size of a door or larger, *stapled* to the gallery wall. Such an unsophisticated presentation was unacceptable in a New York City gallery. If sheets of Plexiglas large enough to cover these massive drawings in a single frame had existed at the time, no one knew about them. Options did exist, but their cost was too high for me to consider. The only affordable option meant cutting a drawing into frameable pieces and presenting them as diptychs or triptychs. The first time a framer did this, he sliced the drawing precisely through its focal point! I wasn't about to let that happen again. The problem forced me to face facts, if I wanted a one-woman show in this woman's gallery, I had to change mediums. This meant I had to return to painting my landscapes in oils on canvas.

Week after week, I attempted to resurrect my oil painting skills, but to no avail. Then, in desperation, I decided to use this exercise to address the problem. When I reached the point of posing these questions to my imaginary spokesperson, what emerged was staggering— the last thing I ever would have expected. It seems the idea I was a failure was something the chorus of three (my mother and two siblings) needed me to keep believing. It was the only way they could keep justifying their warped opinions of me. They needed me to believe I was a failure. As long as my behavior complied with their belief, they could say, "See! We've been right about Cathy all along." According to my imaginary spokesperson, creating bad paintings was for my own good. Affirming this childhood belief was the way my fear could keep me safe. Even though I adopted their belief as a child, as an adult I could choose to think differently about myself. Towards the end of my career as a professional painter, my mother actually expressed an interest in seeing a show of mine that was currently up. When she entered the gallery, she commented, "You did this?" Recognizing that I had believed I was a failure, I had continued believing it as a matter of childhood security pinpointed the obstacle

Good Parenting Part II: Detachment

Like physical wounds, emotional injuries require healing measures specific to the source of the problem. The source of the dysfunctional belief you are investigating can often be found in the memories associated with the fear. This can put an entirely new twist on those memories. The resulting shift in perspective can release resistance.

Please answer any of the following questions that apply to you. These answers help initiate the release of resistance.

- How did my lack of knowledge as a child affect the development of this belief?

- What do I understand now, as an adult, about the situation, myself, or the other people involved at that time? How does viewing these memories through my adult perspective affect them?

- Was a fear of inadequacy, or not being good enough, part of why I adopted this childhood belief?

- Hiding behind this belief has been a form of protection. At the time, what did I feel I needed protection from? Who or why?

- How do these memories affect my current beliefs about myself and others?

Somewhere in your answers to these questions, everything operational fear has been protecting the child you once were from knowing will come to light. Answers to these questions are essential for detaching yourself from the belief you have just exposed. Awareness of these building blocks lays the foundation for healing the belief you have just identified.

Good Parenting Part III: Acceptance and Forgiveness

Fear uses resistance to keep your mind closed. Insights from the previous questions open your mind to acceptance. The ability to accept sets the foundation for the next aspect of the healing process: forgiveness of all the disturbing things your memories unearthed about yourself, the other people who contributed to creating the problem, and God, as strange as it may seem. Answers to those questions play a significant role in achieving forgiveness.

Information you have just unearthed about yourself or other people involved can be beneficial to achieving forgiveness. In all innocence, children often wrongly interpret what people say or do. For instance, my brother and sister were only children themselves at the time. It's hard to imagine a child choosing to join the losing team, let alone befriend an untouchable. Since I was an untouchable and on the losing team, the last thing my brother and sister could have done was defend me. Like all children, they wanted to be on the winning team. Unconsciously, being winners shored up their sense of security. Once this idea finally dawned on me, my attitude shifted. It was easy to forgive my siblings for what I had previously believed was their betrayal.

Human beings make obvious targets to blame for what did or didn't happen, but implicating God? That idea seems to go against the grain. But the truth is, my childhood beliefs about God as a child surprised me.

Thinking him all-powerful, I thought he *could* have prevented the abuse. And too, if God really loved me, he *would* have, or *should* have rescued me, but he didn't. I resented God. He had abandoned me in my hour of need. These immature suspicions prevented me from trusting God. Forgiving God plugged up a hole in my heart that had subliminally always existed, finally making me whole.

Good Parenting Part IV: Gratitude

Once you achieve acceptance and forgiveness, gratitude becomes the next rung on the ladder to healing your belief.

Gratitude is an expression of love. Because fear supports resistance, reaching a point of gratitude is critical to releasing the resistance that operational fear creates. Give yourself plenty of time to thoroughly consider the following questions.

- As a child, how did I benefit from having this belief?
- Since then, how has this belief impacted my life?
- How would my life have been better had I not believed this about myself, my situation, or others?

Much of what we value as adults is based on our past. Mother's cold heart sent me on a life-long quest to understand the ins and outs of love. This has given great purpose to my life. Considering how much my theory surrounding fear flies in the face of tradition, if I had "fit" in and been deemed "acceptable" as a child, I am sure I would have been too afraid to step outside the boundary of beliefs my family found acceptable to write this book. Sticking my neck out therefore was not the threat it might have posed otherwise. The moment I realized how much my life had benefited from being the black sheep of my family, the feeling of gratitude burst within me like a bottle of champagne popping open. The ecstasy I felt then indicated I had finally healed the old belief.

Good Parenting Part V: The Victory Journal

The Victory Journal is the most essential part of the Good Parenting exercise. It is about establishing a new behavior to replace a dysfunctional belief. As I've pointed out, resistance functions robotically. Whether you are twenty or one hundred years old, it will continue treating you as if you are still a child. Without completing this final step, operational fear will resume control and life will continue as before. Several of the people I have worked with whiz through the first parts of this exercise, but just as they begin a Victory Journals, something mysteriously pops up. A grandchild in Alaska gets the whooping cough, and oh, so sorry, I am too worried about her to keep working. Excuses, excuses. The process takes time and effort, but most of all, it takes *total commitment*.

The Victory Journal is the ultimate two-by-four, preventing resistance from worming its way back into your life. As simple as the process appears, it separates the doers from the dabblers. Using the Victory Journal proves you are committed to taking responsibility for yourself, your behavior, and the possible consequences.

For these purposes, find a notebook you can comfortably keep while completing this part or use your Notes app on your phone. Each time you face a situation you are addressing, after completing all of the previous parts, follow these steps:

- Out loud, using the name you gave the fear, thank it for protecting you so well and for so long.

- Express gratitude for the gift(s) it has given you throughout your life.

- And now, firmly say, "I am ready to take control."

- At this point, mindfully choose a behavior that will manifest your desired goal.

- Each time you employ the new behavior, record everything you did in your Victory Journal.

Keep recording each time you replace an old behavior with the new one in your Victory Journal until the new behavior becomes automatic. Said a bit differently, the new behavior *replaces the old behavior.*

The entries in this journal offer undeniable proof of your power to change a behavior. If you ever question your ability to reach your goal, these entries will remind you of what you are capable of, which is the beauty of keeping a Victory Journal.

Almost simple-minded, yes, but don't let the lack of sophistication fool you. This is a powerful tool. One of the first times I worked through the exercise occurred when the gallery in New Your City refused to show my pastels as they were shown in Kentucky. I desperately needed to change mediums. Years before, I had painted in oils, so the transition did not seem problematic. However, after working solely in pastels for so long, to my horror, the transition back to painting became impossible. To make matters worse, never thinking the transition would be a problem, I had consented to have a one-woman show in Louisville a year later. After wasting several months failing to paint decent paintings, I was frantic. The opening was only ten months away when I addressed the problem using this exercise.

The fear obstructing my efforts turned out to be Agnes' taunts and Mother's blatant assessment of my abilities. As a teenager, when I told her I might major in art in college, she said it was a good choice because, "People who lack the intelligence to do anything else become artists." Was I genuinely unintelligent, and the failure they had convinced me I was? Of course not! However, I was paralyzed with these messages unconsciously looping around in my head.

When I confronted the fear in Step Six of Part One, asking questions of the fear, the answer came out as a sneer that sounded as if it were coming directly out of Agnes' mouth! Amazing. Once I had a handle on the fear, every time I felt the cringe picking up a paintbrush, I repeated the steps outlined in this part and recorded the actions I took in my Victory Journal. In ten months, I produced eight paintings, which for me was a fantastic feat. All that were for sale, sold.

The next exercise is based on simple memories. Even though it is less involved than the Good Parenting exercise, the results can be profound.

Exercise #2: The Healing Perspective

Some of the most innocent childhood misconceptions can morph into monumental problems in adulthood if they remain under wraps. Simply telling someone about a childhood experience can be healing in itself. I will never forget the relief I felt when I finally confessed to my psychiatrist a profoundly shameful secret I had held onto since childhood. I had tortured earthworms by dropping them into bonfires I made with kitchen matches several times. My psychiatrist was incredulous. "Earthworms? You are upset because you roasted earthworms?" His lack of revulsion flabbergasted me. In my mind, what I had done was so loaded with the anger and the shame it represented about conflicts with Agnes that it had inflated the memory to epic proportions. Taking the secret out of the closet and reviewing the story behind it as an adult put the memory in proper perspective.

Many unintentional events can cause lifelong damage when left unresolved. A fifty-year-long battle between my father's sisters was just such a situation. The basis of this battle was a common enough: preparation for a family photograph. My grandmother understandably wanted her four daughters to look their best. Three of her daughters had curly hair, one did not. For this reason, their mother focused her attention on curling the hair of the straight-haired daughter. One of the curly-haired sisters misinterpreted her mother's lack of attention as favoritism towards her other sister. This misguided, immature interpretation kept festering—resentment escalated. Jealously kept this sister picking her scab of bitterness. Her resentment created a lifelong animosity toward her sisters and anyone else this woman feared might outshine her. At any time across the years, had one of the sisters ever dared revisit the situation and openly discussed it with her siblings, I expect a large amount of animosity could have been avoided.

Part One: The Healing Perspective

The Healing Perspective exercise begins with addressing an actual memory. It differs from the previous exercise that started with focusing on a problem, revealing the unconscious fear and the belief it was supporting, then replacing that dysfunctional belief and its behavior with a new, positive behavior and belief. In this exercise, thinking about a childhood incident, the fear and the belief it generated become obvious. The result of questioning yourself about this past experience in light of the following questions can produce amazing results.

Take any childhood memory that comes to mind and ask yourself these questions:

- When this event happened, what were the immediate consequences?

- How did the experience make me feel?

- What emotions did the situation elicit?

- What belief did I take away from the experience?

- How has this belief impacted my adult life?

- How have I benefited from having had this belief?

This exercise was especially effective for a woman who had volunteered to work with me as I experimented with ideas for this book. Whenever Elsie and I met, she complained about "her stupid family." She was especially critical of her older sister, whom she characterized as a whiny victim and ruthless manipulator—just like their mother. She hated them both.

One day, while musing about her childhood, Elsie told me about the ugly, dirty clothes she had to wear to school. Elsie said if her mother had loved her, she would have provided Elsie with cleaner, better clothes. The shame and embarrassment her clothes caused Elsie were bad enough, but the added insult of her classmates making fun of her clothing left her feeling ostracized. As a consequence, Elsie became a loner.

When I asked her how she might have benefited from being an outcast, she realized being a loner had proven to be positive. Identifying as a loner allowed her to disassociate herself from her family's values and behaviors. Unburdened by the need to fit in, Elsie virtually threw herself out of the nest. Consequently, Elsie had unparalleled freedom to adopt a healthier mindset, which her older sister never did. According to Elsie this was why her sister ended up being so much like their mother, while she did not.

Once Elsie realized how much she had benefited from her past, her attitude altered. This shift led to two incredible changes. Her sense of separation vanished, and her opinions about her sister and mother completely changed. The next time Elsie and I met, she told me about a recent event that took my breath away. In the weeks between our visits, she invited her once-despised sister to accompany her on a retreat. If that wasn't impressive enough, Elsie reported that, for the first time in her life, she enjoyed being with her sister.

Even positive incidents can reveal helpful information. On several weekends as a child, my first keeper, Nettie, took me with her when she visited her family on their farm. I loved these visits, as they provided so many fascinating experiences I had never encountered at home. In my high school yearbook, which I had long forgotten, I am quoted as saying my life's dream is to live on a farm and raise chickens. So, it should not have come as a surprise that when Ken and I purchased a farm in 1989, unconsciously drawn by those happy memories, I later discovered we had bought a farm within five miles of Nettie's homestead! The chickens never appeared, but I did raise peacocks.

The events of the past cannot change. Only our perspective about them can, and changing that can be redemptive. The pity is that so many of us insist on living our lives while self-righteously hanging on to destructive childhood conceits, as my father's sisters did. Instead of risking falling off an incredibly gratifying high horse, many of us, like cows, prefer chewing the cud of a resentment. We prefer to feed divisiveness over peace, to separate ourselves from people we love by championing our denunciations, justifications, and rationalizations. Cossetted attitudes like these only shore up our immature selves; therefore, we remain as inept and ineffectual when we become adults as we were when we were children.

It is the rare child who escapes their early years unscathed. For sure, some children suffer more than others. The spectrum of suffering is endless: the six-year-old Rwandan child, forced by war out of her home to tread a seemingly infinite journey of strife and starvation; the Jewish child during World War II, ripped from the arms of his parents, never to see them again; the precious toddler victimized by a pedophile uncle; the five-year-old boy, who left to his own devices, discovers a pack of matches and for the first time strikes one. Horrified, he drops the flaming stick on the carpet and helplessly runs from the blaze, only to be later accused of killing his sister when the house burns down with her inside. *Every human being* is scarred one way or another—even the boy raised by the most loving human beings ever wrote that his worst experience was being forced to attend cotillion classes.

Childhood problems provide a wall that supports the emotional growth needed to become responsible, compassionate adults. This requires only one thing; the courage to revisit your past wounds. In offering the Good

Parenting and Healing Perspective exercises, I hope to help you turn past events into fodder for emotional and, therefore, spiritual growth as opposed to allowing them to continue generating conflict and ruining your life.

If you recall, resistance continually works to prevent detection. It all hinges on awareness. Since most internal conflicts appear highly disguised, some of them have already sneaked into your life and you don't even know it. As happened to the protagonist in *The Truman Show*, the key to freedom is recognizing events in your life, or ways of behaving that have been causing conflict, but so subtly, they have gone unrecognized. To help you with this recognition process, the next chapter explores some of the disguises I have identified to date. Since we are all different, you may have disguises unique to you. Hopefully, reading about some of these will trigger a memory of one of yours.

Chapter 12

Veiled Conflicts

This chapter covers some covert disguises of operational fear that I have discovered to date. By no means is this list complete. Considering each person is unique, so will be the disguises that outgrown beliefs take that prevent emotional, and therefore, spiritual growth. Familiarity with these disguises can at least sensitize you to the issue.

The Gift of Conflict

Because the goal of unconscious fear is to protect us, it will do everything within its power to deter detection. For example, whenever I was a pleaser, I felt a tightening in my throat. Was that feeling expressing resistance? Absolutely, but had I not delved into this subject, I would never have discovered its significance. Due to its ability to camouflage expressions of internal conflicts, resistance poses the greatest obstacle to emotional and therefore, spiritual growth. The more I understand the inner workings of operational fear, the easier it has been to detect covert signs of resistance that it is generating.

Conflicts present pregnant prospects for growth. Every day, we encounter internal conflicts, but more often than not, these instances go unnoticed. Sometimes it's because our culture has incorporated these expressions as part of the cultural norm—people claim they are just the way life is. Other times, they appear so well camouflaged no one pays them attention. When our egos fixate on a sense of righteousness, the temptation is to ignore the fact that resistance is causing the fixation. In order to become more powerfully effective individuals and grow spiritually, becoming attuned to the expression of concealed conflict is important.

Even though most conflicts are unique to an individual, there are many we share in common. Many appear cloaked in similar costumes. The following examples illustrate the common, clandestine ways I have discovered that expose the unconscious fears that lead us astray. Familiarity with these examples and some of the accepted cultural ways of behaving, which are, in truth, signs of operational fear in disguise, will hopefully make it easier for you to identify the conflicts blocking your growth. Here are some common disguises of operational fear that foment conflict.

- Uncharacteristic behaviors
- Euphemisms
- "Shoulds"
- Judging strangers
- Baseless accusations
- Uncharacteristic thoughts
- Extreme discomfort
- Shame and guilt
- Inappropriate actions
- Obsessions

- Belonging
- Prejudices
- Expectations and assumptions
- Excuses
- Attachments or preoccupations
- Rumination or irritability
- "Buttons"
- Unfounded envy
- Sin
- Being different
- Unconscious needs
- "White lies"
- Dwelling on past events
- The inability to admit you are in the wrong

Let's take a closer look at each of these.

Uncharacteristic Behaviors

To save money, a friend and I pooled resources to rent an art studio in a newly renovated building. Putting the two of us together in the same room must have been one of the best jokes the gods had pulled off in eons. Ellen is a self-proclaimed perfectionist in everything—personal looks, home, behavior, husband, even children! And then there's me. I am too spontaneous to worry about being perfect.

Soon after we took possession of the studio, the joke surfaced when we learned there would be an official opening of the building. City officials, wine, cheese, reporters—the whole shebang. To prepare for this big event, Ellen and I decided to paint the walls of our studio together. Oh boy! At the appointed hour we began painting; me in my corner, Ellen in hers. I was so engrossed in what I was doing that it took me a while to become aware of Ellen's admonishments to herself. "Darn it all," she kept repeating. "I keep dripping paint. Why am I dripping paint all over the place? This isn't like me at all!"

Wow! Those words brought me up sharp. I was not only fascinated, but er, well, truth be told, I confess to being a tad tickled. I, the slob, had not dripped one spot of paint, while Ellen, it seemed, couldn't stop dribbling paint. Then, if that wasn't enough, the poor woman managed to tip the entire contents of her paint can onto the floor. Her exclamation, "This isn't like me at all!" couldn't have made the issue more evident.

When someone like Ellen does something contrary to their character in this way, we assume the person is just having a bad day. Having just learned what this type of behavior indicates in my Jungian class, I had reason to believe Ellen's uncharacteristic behavior was an expression of an outgrown belief that only Ellen could ever identify. The tipoff lay in the words, "This isn't like me at all."

The belief that was causing this odd behavior is not for me to say. As a thought, at this stage of Ellen's life, perfectionism may have been boxing her in, limiting her potential. Had she been interested in growing spiritually, recognizing her odd behavior as an indicator of an internal conflict would have been a gift.

Euphemisms

Because emotional outbursts are disturbing, we are taught from an early age to conceal emotions with pleasantries. On his radio show, *The Prairie Home Companion,*

Garrison Keillor turned this pickle into an anthropological phenomenon as it occurs in Minnesota. According to Keillor, no one in Minnesota ever expects an honest answer to civilities such as, "How are you?" The answer is always, "Oh, fine, just fine," even if the speaker's wife just ran off with the milkman. Having been married to a Minnesotan, I assure you this is the case. Minnesotans rarely call a spade a spade.

During the early, tumultuous years of my marriage to Ken, if anyone dared suggest I was angry with him, I would have been appalled. Doormats never get angry; they deserve whatever life dishes up for them. The fact I knew I was furious but couldn't admit it should have alerted me to the fact I had a problem that needed my attention. But no, I was never angry, just disappointed. These temperate expressions of anger allow dysfunctional childhood beliefs such as mine and the resulting behaviors to remain incognito.

Euphemisms used to conceal emotions, particularly anger, are the worst offenders. Even though you might be downright angry with a person, you would never outright tell them that. Heavens no! Instead, you tell them they hurt your feelings or something to that effect. Unless anger is explosively expressed, it is rare to hear it honestly expressed.

Because Mother was never angry, she thought she could claim she was a real "lady." The idea that ladies were never angry was integral to her identity. Her notions about anger forced its expression underground, surfacing as passive-aggressive behavior.

"Shoulds"

"Shoulds" or "supposed tos" often reflect beliefs or social mores that we have simply adopted without ever knowing it. If ever they were, they may no longer be appropriate or applicable. Whenever you notice a "should" cropping up in your thoughts or conversations, like when you think you should go to some event that you are not interested in, always check to make sure your values are in sync with the purpose of what you are doing.

The last thirty years have wiped clean the slate of "shoulds" I grew up with. Children should be seen and not heard; a woman's place is in the home; marriage is between a man and a woman. My children's generation freed themselves from many cultural shoulds I grew up with. I can't take credit for this change since, without knowing it, I relied on my parents' template as the marriage model. I was the partner who cooked, shopped, and cared for the house and children. Hubby cared for the yard, fixed things, and was always home at six-thirty for supper. Because we both remained true to our parents' models, it generated several problems. After fifteen years of marriage and one gargantuan blow-up, it was apparent that we had been applying two different models to our own marriage. Ken had his. I had mine.

Why this problem didn't come up earlier seems odd, but I suspect, like most couples, we were probably too involved with getting used to living with each other for it to surface earlier. While marital roles aren't the monumental issues that money, religion, or children cause, many conflicts could be avoided if these roles were discussed at the beginning of a relationship.

Judging Strangers

My family had just settled into our seats at the opera when the couple seated before us caught my attention. From how the woman was flirting with her companion, I was sure the couple was on their first date. As I continued to observe them, I became convinced the woman was at least my age, and, on a date with a man my son's age! "What a hussy," I hissed in Ken's ear, "clowning around so outrageously." I became so engrossed with the activities in the row in front of me that I missed most of the opera. It was not until after the performance ended and we were descending the staircase did the realization dawn.

My musings about the woman's behavior revealed something about myself I had yet to recognize. As a child, acting like a clown was my way of getting attention and gaining acceptance. As is the usual case, this belief unconsciously accompanied me into adulthood. Whenever I wanted to impress someone, I reverted to this childhood ploy of clowning around—precisely what I had criticized the woman at the opera for doing. Clowning rarely worked; it turned people off. This realization unmasked a behavior that was no longer serving my best interests. This recognition allowed me to address the belief and remove the operational aspect of fear at its root.

Baseless Accusations

If you've ever tried reasoning with someone caught up in a frenzy of emotion, you know there is nothing you can say or do at that moment that will have an impact. One day, as I stood up to teach the high school Sunday school class, before I opened my mouth one of the boys began throwing accusations at me. According to him, "People like you" (me) were responsible for the riots in Northern Ireland—which was quite a stretch.

While the boy's outburst was disturbing and spurious, the fact he began his accusation with the words, "People like you" made it clear his rant had nothing to do with me. In all probability, it reflected a problem he needed to address.

Uncharacteristic Thoughts

Years ago, a woman told me about an incident that happened to her when she was still a nun. At the time, she felt that her current assignment was not a good fit for her. She especially disliked the constant travel the position required. Nevertheless, being the good nun that she was, she never complained. Then, one day after checking into yet another hotel, upon entering her new room, she wandered over to the window to survey the view. Spotting an ordinary-looking woman standing on the street below, the thought came to the nun, "What a whore!"

The nun couldn't believe such a thought had popped into her head about a woman she had never seen before. Stricken, she sat down to consider where such a random idea had come from. It didn't take long for the source of the thought to surface. By staying in her present assignment, she felt she was *prostituting* herself. As peculiar as the idea was, it was spot-on—an ingenious expression of a belief that had been limiting her. Until then, she believed she had to accept whatever assignment she was handed and never object. In the past, that had worked, but no longer. Shortly afterwards, the nun requested reassignment to a job better suited to her natural inclinations.

Extreme Discomfort

The best example of this camouflage is what happened to me when the Episcopal seminary student I mentioned earlier fell in love with me during freshman year in college. The guy actually fell in love with me, the spurned black sheep of the family! What was he thinking? With the doormat calling the shots, I was not worthy of such deep affection. Ironically, all I had ever dreamt of was a knight in shining armor showing up to rescue me, someone exactly like Albert. However, when my knight appeared, I could not handle his admiration. His love contradicted everything I unconsciously believed about myself. His total acceptance distressed me to such an extent I ran away from him as fast as I could, as if my life depended on it— which, in light of my issues then, it probably did.

The foreign nature of Albert's adoration felt threatening. Repulsions like this one are prime indicators of internal conflicts yet to be recognized. Unfortunately for Albert, it took me years to acknowledge this dysfunctional belief.

Shame and Guilt

Having had the idea drilled into my head that my problems with Agnes were my fault shame, and guilt became an integral part of my thoughts. This became especially problematic after I married Ken. Unbeknownst to either of us, Ken had an unconscious compulsion to serve his clients and parents first, my needs as a wife and mother always came second. But who was I to complain? I was lucky if he came home to eat supper before returning to the office.

After one of his unbearably painful absences, we took our children to a state park for a picnic to compensate for his lack of presence. One of my sons took a picture of Ken and me that day. Looking at my face, no one would ever have guessed the depth of anger I felt then. I had become such a good actor. As a doormat, it was almost impossible for me to demand better treatment for myself. Shame and guilt over the knife incident with Agnes zipped my mouth shut, locking me into a life that was, by all accounts, miserable.

Inappropriate Actions

One of the ways I protected myself as a child was to set myself apart from my family; therefore, I became programmed to be a loner. Much later, when I realized I had met someone I wanted to befriend, I would find myself uttering the perfect comment or acting in the exact way to put the person off—never consciously doing so. It surprises me how I always knew exactly what to say or do to repel a particular person so I could remain true to myself as a loner.

Even now, reaching out to another person in a way that might connect us still feels intimidating. Because I am now aware of this fear, it no longer is able to affect my behavior.

Obsessions

As I pointed out earlier, Mother had a "thing" about fat people. When I was eight years old, I weighed 52 pounds. Mother found this unacceptable. She bribed me with the promise of my first watch if I lost four pounds, which I dutifully did.

Fat was her barometer of acceptability. The first thing Mother ever noticed about another person was their weight. Mother's obsession with fat people was an unconscious expression of fear from her teenage days when she was overweight. Obsessions, fixations—any subject that raises a person's hackles, like weight, race, or politics, stand out as red flags indicating an unconscious belief that needs to be exhumed and transformed by way of the exercises just given.

Belonging

The idea of belonging seems to be an intrinsic part of the human experience. Our children belong to us. This sweater belongs to you. And as I pointed out earlier, the reason I adopted my family's beliefs came from my need to feel I belonged—all seemingly innocuous. Nevertheless, belonging has a dark side due to the unconscious security it offers.

Once, a committed young preacher served in a church in Waddy, Kentucky, for a short period. The man could not say enough against homosexuals. According to him, they didn't belong in our church. When I questioned him about his conviction, he admitted his parents vehemently rejected homosexuals. The root of his anti-Christian mindset was the same as the one that fed my prejudice against greedy people: the unconscious childhood fear of parental rejection. The young preacher was so attached to needing his parents' approval that fear of losing it unconsciously trumped Christ's only commandment admonition in Matthew 7:1 to "Judge not that ye be not judged." Love unites. Judgments divide people, separating "them" from "us."

The need to belong can wreak unconscionable atrocities. As an undercurrent theme, belonging has seeded most of our wars. A prime example is the Hatfield-McCoy feud that occurred in the Cumberland area of eastern Kentucky is. According to Harry M. Caudill, author of *Night Comes to the Cumberlands,* [9] the Civil War gave rise to these interfamily feuds. Even though the war was over when the feuds began, when one member in a family, who had belonged to the Union, met up with a neighbor who had supported the Confederate, conflict ensued. According to Caudill, diabolical, "monstrous adventures in homicide…were virtually self-perpetuating." Neighbors burned down each other's homes, stole their livestock and in some instances, shot families as they ran from their burning houses only to have the same thing done to them by someone wanting revenge.

Prejudice

A prejudice is just a belief that's simply been adopted. The holder of that belief has never had the personal experience that produces other beliefs. Strangely enough, my dogs' behavior offers the perfect illustration of how a prejudice comes into being and is perpetuated. At one time, we owned two German shepherds who were sisters, Rita and Fonzene, plus a small terrier, Amos. One icy winter night, when I let the three dogs out for the last time that day, Fonzene, with Rita at her side, suddenly attacked Amos on the porch. My desperate attempts to rescue Amos finally worked long enough for me to haul the sisters back into the house. Amos managed to drag himself off the porch during my short absence and away from the house.

When I went out to help him, Amos was nowhere to be found; no trail of blood, no trace of him whatsoever. Alone, on the darkest night, with Ken out of town, I was in hysterics. Worse, the batteries in my flashlight were too old and weak to be of use. Desperate to find Amos, I phoned our neighbors to help me. Even with the aid of additional lights, we couldn't find him.

Fonzene, who I thought instigated the attack, went to a new home the next day. Rita, who hadn't appeared to be as involved in the attack as her sister, stayed.

Because I had been in hysterics when I used the phone the night of the attack, anytime the phone rang, or

I used it thereafter, Rita went into a tizzy. She associated the frenzy I was in the night Amos died with phones. Six weeks later, we brought a German shepherd puppy into our fold. Rita and the puppy, Sassy Maude, were together for only a year before I realized Rita shared the same bloodlust as her sister, so she went to a new home. (Fortunately, where we lived, German shepherds were in high demand as guard dogs.) Nevertheless, for the year they were together, Rita conveyed her fear of telephones to Sassy Maude by how she reacted when our phone rang.

Five years after Rita's departure, Sassy Maude still ran away when the phone rang. Soon after we moved to Minnesota and got another shepherd puppy. After two months with us, the puppy started showing signs that he had adopted Sassy's fear of landline phones (cell phones didn't count, thank heavens). The puppy's reaction to phones was a type of prejudice—no experience, just a belief that has been adopted. In this case, a behavior that had originated years before he was born with Rita's reactions to ringing telephones.

Expectations and Assumptions

Each human being, even members of the same family, grows up under unique circumstances. As I mentioned earlier, my sister never stopped refusing to believe the stories I told about my experiences with Agnes. They never happened to her, so they couldn't have happened to me. The individuality of our perspectives must always be taken into account. Someone I know once quipped that if there were only two people on earth, there would be two religions.

Because we experience life filtered through our unique perspectives, they affect the beliefs our experiences create. Conflict becomes inevitable when our unique perspectives lead us to make erroneous assumptions about other people's words or actions.

Excuses

The perfect example of the use of this camouflage is the woman mentioned earlier who said she was too busy to take up painting. The woman's excuse expressed an unconscious fear, the root of her internal conflict.

Attachments or Preoccupations

If there ever was an example of an ambiguous camouflage, it is money. The lack of money is commonly attributed to conditions, chance, or fate. While for some people this is true, in many cases the root of money problems has more to do with parental attitudes about money that a child adopts.

By generating detrimental behaviors that perpetuate the lack of funds, beliefs about the lack of money can become self-perpetuating. My conditioning could have convinced me I deserved to be poor. In the same way that my doormat convinced me I was unlovable to the extent I was unable to accept love, had I believed I deserved to be poor, my behavior would have unconsciously worked to keep me poor.

When I discovered my religious upbringing had created a fear of wealth that was unconsciously influencing me, I was shocked. Like many Christians, I interpreted Christ's invitation to Matthew, the tax collector, to leave his money behind and follow him as a statement against wealth. This led me to believe I could not be a highly spiritual person and wealthy at the same time, that having money was bad. After exploring how unconscious fear affects behavior, I realized Christ's request of Matthew probably had little to do with money. It was about attachments. Was having money more important to Matthew than the prospect of the spiritual wealth he would gain by following Christ? Had Matthew been attached to his wealth, it would have prevented him from becoming a disciple. As things turned out, following Christ was more important to Matthew than his wealth. Thus, he was able to turn his back on his former life.

If Christ came to me this minute and told me to give up my wealth and follow him, without hesitation I would jump at the invitation. On the other hand, if Christ had come to me forty years ago and asked me to give up coffee and follow him, that would have been the last thing I could have done. I was so addicted to coffee that, before such appliances were available, I had rigged up a timer on a coffee maker in our bedroom so I could have a hot cup of coffee while still in bed, coffee was that important to me.

Life was copacetic until the summer of the two tornados. The first storm occurred in Louisville and took out electricity in our area for an entire week. Seven days without morning coffee turned me into a viper of the first order. As those were pre-Starbucks days, it wasn't until I made it to the delicatessen next to my studio and downed that all-important cup of hot coffee that life became bearable. That same summer, while on vacation in Michigan, a second tornado touched down close to the cottage we were renting. For five days the electricity was down in the entire area. Getting that vital fix of hot coffee required that I drive forty-five minutes to the closest café that still had electricity! I was miserable beyond belief.

Was I suffering because I had lost an arm, my eyesight, or perhaps a family member? No. The source of my agony came from the absence of hot coffee first thing in the morning! Coffee? I found it to be an abomination that something as insignificant as coffee could control my life to this extent. My reactions to the absence of coffee alerted me to the fact I was addicted to the stuff. As a consequence, I became determined to rectify the problem. It took me nine months, but I did it! Strangely, I found eliminating coffee was much harder than giving up cigarettes even though very few people would ever treat it as being as addictive as alcohol due to its popularity and, maybe more importantly, the profits of the industries that rely on its popularity. Regardless, never again was I going to allow something as insignificant as coffee to rule my life.

If certain things or habits are essential to your well-being, in all probability, it's an attachment. Mother's preoccupation with maintaining her cherished, limited life would have been as impossible for her to give up as my reliance on coffee was for me. The unconscious beliefs that back attachments become the obstacles to emotional and therefore spiritual growth.

Identifying attachments can be problematic, considering they have become an intrinsic part of your life for so long. Universal acceptance of things like coffee clouds the issue. The tricky aspect is realizing you have a problem.

When I imagined Christ coming to me and asking me to give up coffee and follow him, the question exposed the attachment. I've also discovered negative attachments when something is lost or taken away along with disruptions to the usual way of life. Even small attachments, as insignificant as they may appear, can reveal how much my sense of security relies on truly meaningless things which can be blocking my ability to grow spiritually.

Rumination or Irritability

Gnawing a thought to death as in ruminating over aspects of a conversation, or suddenly finding myself in a grumpy mood for no apparent reason indicates an internal conflict. In the past, whenever I found myself trying to justify something I have done, I began ruminating about it, maybe even for days. Then I discovered the cure. By finding a secluded place where I can confess out loud to myself that what I did or said was inappropriate or wrong, the mental wrangling magically stops. With resistance no longer clogging my brain, I can accept responsibility for my action and begin investigating the originating fear.

"Buttons"

Contrary to popular assumption, when you accuse someone of "pushing your buttons," that someone is not the problem. In truth, you have an issue causing you to react by blaming it on someone else. Labeling these reactions "buttons" is an ingenious way to deflect responsibility. The idea of accusing someone of pushing your buttons relieves you of having to own your problem. As with ruminations, use of the "button" metaphor is a surefire sign of an outgrown belief that is no longer working in your best interests.

Unfounded Fears

If a screeching monkey once pounced on your head and woke you up in the wee hours one morning, as once happened to me, then a fear of monkeys is not indicative of an unconscious fear. I have never been in an airplane accident; nevertheless, for the first four decades of my live I had a white-knuckle fear of flying. By happenstance, in 1983, the problem disappeared when inadvertently I eliminated the source of the problem.

The day I visited Agnes in her nursing home with my psychiatrist, nothing substantive was achieved other than the visit convinced my doctor I had been telling him the truth about my past. The encounter left me profoundly disturbed. As far as I was concerned, nothing significant had been accomplished. In desperation, I sought the help of the minister of my church.

According to him, Agnes' accusations, aided by my siblings' accusations and Mother's indifference, had turned me into the family scapegoat. I was all alone—*powerless*, without the means to control my life in any way. Even though by confronting Agnes I felt I had been "heard" (maybe not as much by Agnes as my psychiatrist), nothing changed. I was still as impotent as I had been all my life. A day later, following an overwhelming impulse, I phoned Agnes. The conversation had barely started when, as I recall, I mentioned something about our past. Again, Agnes dismissed everything as being totally insignificant. Her apathy was beyond belief. Exasperated, I responded by saying, "Three people know the truth about what happened between us...you, me, and God, who you will soon have to face and I wish you all the luck in the world. Goodbye."

Saying this to Agnes caused a seismic shift in my head. My body felt unfamiliar. For many days that followed, it took me an hour to decide what clothes to put on my body, even though I consistently wore a uniform of jeans and a T-shirk to work.

A few weeks later, Ken and I flew to France. We had been airborne for an hour when I suddenly realized the plane had taken off. I had not noticed. My fear of flying was gone! My unmitigated inability to control my destiny as a child had been manifesting as a fear of flying. Shifting responsibility for everything off my shoulders and onto where it had belonged all along vanquished my childhood fear of being powerless. At last, I was in control of my life.

No amount of sensitivity training could have eliminated my unsubstantiated fear of flying as it can for other people. I suspect any attempt to school out my fear of flying before would have simply shifted how and where my childhood fear of being powerless would have reappeared. And reappear it would have. Fear will unconsciously generate dysfunctional reactions until the core belief is rooted out and dealt with.

Sin

The concept of sin is solely religious, a violation of the will of God or divine law. Behaviors that hurt, kill, or maim living beings can be labeled reprehensible, pernicious, may even being labeled evil, but again they are evil or sinful only from a religious perspective. While injurious behaviors might fit the definition of evil, in truth, the force that causes sinful, evil behaviors is not the devil. If it suits you, call all it the devil, but true cause of these behaviors is operational fear. Operational fear alone is responsible for behaviors that religions label sinful, or evil.

According to religious dogma, the concept of sin means separation from God. Realistically, though, I have to wonder how beings of spirit can ever be separated from God. The fact is, it is an impossibility. Having been created in God's image as spiritual beings, separation from our spirit as the concept of sin implies is a blatant contradiction. When fear no longer existed as a mere awareness in Adam and Eve's minds, and turned into an unconscious, operational factor, the switch caused a tectonic shift in the way they perceived all of life. This shift caused two effects: they began believing they were separated from God. In turn, their new-found perception of separation lead to the concept of dichotomy—as in good and evil.

What I intended to do the day I held a knife above Agnes's head is still unclear. Scare her enough to treat me better, absolutely, but kill her? Never. Without question, what I did was a mistake, one that shows sufficient pressure can force anyone to take such drastic actions, but was it a sin? At the time I believed it was a sin. Labeling it as a sin bolted me into hopeless subjugation as a sinner. Because she knew she would be fired if word got out about what had happened, Agnes made me promise never to tell anyone about the incident. She needn't have worried. The guilt I suffered thinking I was a sinner handcuffed me to unshakable shame.

As the years passed, without a means to rectify the psychological underpinnings of what had prompted me to take such an unconscionable action, believing the behavior to be sinful, guilt and shame festered. A healthy relationship with God became impossible. There was no question in my mind "[I am]...not worthy so much as to gather up the crumbs under that Table" (a sentence taken from a communion prayer once part of Episcopal services). Considering the hopelessness of my situation, the idea that I was a sinner locked me into the belief that I was separated from God's love.

However, once I substituted the word "mistake" for "sin," the switch unlocked my brain. As a mistake, I was free to discover and heal the underlying problem. Years later, my therapist (not the old psychiatrist) told me that at that time in my life, considering all I was dealing with, holding a knife above Agnes' head was possibly the healthiest action I took.

Admitting you have sinned is as effective as putting a bandage over an untreated wound. Without addressing the unconscious fear operating to trigger the mistake/sin, the underlying fear will keep festering, creating an ever-increasing number of problems.

By whatever name you call it, be it sin or mistake, eradicating such a problem requires dealing with the fear initiating the behavior. Most of the actions we label as sins are merely mistakes seeded by misguided, inaccurate understanding, childhood experiences and the like. To be sure, some are far worse than others, horrendous, unimaginably brutal. The people that commit these crimes need to be kept in jail to keep the rest of us safe. But imagine how different life would be if, one day, the word "mistake" replaced the word "sin." By substituting the word "mistake" for "sin," the ability to rectify one of these behaviors becomes an option not otherwise possible.

Being Different

My mind tends to treat anything that differs too widely from information not already included in my Primer for life 101 as a bogeyman. The automatic association of "different" with danger is understandable, but all too often, the outcomes that this unconscious association foments are tragic. Knowing the extent of trauma it has caused—saying it's ironic knowing the root of these behaviors is merely a psychological parent's attempt to preserve the immature child it first appeared to protect seems like a grievously shallow statement however true it is.

Antagonism against anything or anyone deemed different, from ugly dogs to Jews, Democrats, Republicans, Muslims, Mexicans, or people who go on picnics, is representative of the unconscious effects of resistance at their worst.

Unconscious Needs

Needs that fear unconsciously sustains can go well beyond food and shelter, as the following example will show. Years ago, I committed one of the worst violations against another person. I violated a woman's trust by exposing her secret. This woman and I only met once on vacation. When her husband's work brought them to town, she looked me up, and we spent a day together. During that time, she confided in me that she was having an affair. Even though I welcomed the intimacy, I found her confession strangely nauseating.

That evening at dinner with our spouses, I "accidentally" spilled the beans to her spouse. I would love to claim that the second *after* I exposed her infidelity, I realized I had done something unforgivable. The truth is, in the back of my mind, I knew what I was doing. I needed to do it, but I was clueless about *why* I would do such a loathsome thing. After years of berating myself, I finally exhumed the basis of this conflict. The impulse arose from an unconscious need to protect my father.

Years before Daddy died, he began exhibiting symptoms of Parkinson's disease. Mother could not handle seeing the Viking she had married disintegrate into a needy, helpless man. The sicker he got, the more vodka she drank. Mother virtually abandoned Daddy to grieve the disintegration of his body alone. The loss of his identity as a powerful leader was bad enough, but the lack of compassion and support from the most important person in his life was heartbreaking.

At the time, I was living in Chicago. On my last visit, Daddy was desperate for someone to listen to him, to hear him express what he was feeling through the drool he was incapable of controlling. This Mother couldn't stomach.

So, when my acquaintance confessed her infidelity, in my mind, her indiscretion became Mother's abandonment of Daddy. In effect, I was protecting Daddy when I exposed the woman's secret. Not an excuse at all, but at least I understood why I had so profoundly wronged my friend. I so wish I had been able to apologized to her. Even though immediately afterward it felt like shards of glass filled my stomach because resistance blinded me to the crime I had committed.

Some needs are genuine; however, what we think we need comes from an unconscious need to protect, as was the case just described, or to conform. Marketers have turned us into a nation of unrestrained need by cleverly cultivating our insecurities and exploiting the unconscious need to conform. This can lead to ridiculous ends.

On a day when school was canceled due to heavy snowfall, I was probably the only mother insane enough to leave the safety of home to buy my daughter a particular Cabbage Patch Kid she insisted she *had* to have *that* day. Advertisements on television had brainwashed Maggie into believing the dolls would sell out if I did not get to the store that day when they were first available. If you question this, think about your children's needs compared to those Daniel Boone's children might have had—no Cabbage Patch dolls, for sure.

Imagine how different the world would be without fear continually generating the urge for more and more material wealth regardless of the fact we already have more than we could ever use, all to satisfy our childhood sense of insecurity.

"White Lies"

While nursing my babies, in the quiet of warm afternoons to prevent me from falling asleep and smothering them,

I began watching soap operas. Make all the fun you want of soap operas, but I learned a huge lesson watching the now-defunct soap opera, *The Guiding Light*. After years of watching Reva (yes, once I began watching, I was hooked), the super-glamourous star of the show, tell one white lie after another, the inevitability of the consequences clear. Every lie she told backfired, always with negative repercussions. Did that ever stop Reva? Never. She kept justifying her lies by saying she was protecting this or that person. After years of watching the show, the fact Reva never caught on drove me crazy. Now that I think about it, it was probably a ploy the producers used to keep their audience captivated. It sure kept my attention.

The obvious repercussions of Reva's lies made me question my own white lies. I wondered what would happen if I stopped telling these seemingly innocuous half-truths. The first time I exposed the raw truth about myself I learned several important lessons. While half-truths seem harmless enough, and for the most part they are, when we tell them we are actually damaging ourselves. They reinforce unconscious negative childhood beliefs we still hold about ourselves. As a form of self-protection, we tell these half-truths to cover up our perceived shortcomings. The fact I couldn't face my inadequacies, I assumed I would never have a friend if people knew the real me; therefore, I enhanced the image of the person I showed to others.

Contrary to this assumption, I found openness made me more approachable. People have no problem relating to imperfection; however, perfection puts us on a pedestal that sets us apart. Additionally, the message white lies send to other people is equally problematic. Inadvertently, these lies convey a lack of confidence in the other person's ability to handle the truth. Finally, white lies are divisive. This was an ongoing problem for Reva.

Dwelling on Past Events

Continuing to dwell on something that happened long ago often indicates an unconscious attachment. If you are still agonizing over the money you lost in the stock market ten years ago, it would be wise to investigate your rumination as an internal conflict.

"Bad" things happen naturally. When they do, suffering and mourning are healthy responses. Society accepts victimhood as a natural state, and to a limited degree, it is. However, childhood experiences can establish an unconscious *need* to suffer when it becomes part of our identity. Then, like my doormat, victimhood determines the course of a person's life. In the same way I sought abusive situations as an adult, some people find the familiarity of victimhood comforting.

Long ago, I met a woman who, as a teenager, got pregnant. Fearing what her Catholic parents would do if they discovered she had gotten pregnant out of wedlock, she chose to have an abortion. While the procedure allowed her to escape her parents' retribution, it could not free her from having to deal with her religious upbringing. Over the years, a deep-rooted sense of guilt blossomed in the woman, growing exponentially as she aged. This generated an unconscious need to be punished. Her need for punishment became an ever-present dynamic, manifesting as a pattern of behavior that ruled the rest of her life.

Invariably, just as she was verging on happiness, the woman would suffer a dramatic setback, a weird accident that affected only her, never anyone else. For forty years, her unconscious need to be punished kept her rollercoastering from one improbable accident to another. Keeping her abortion a secret may have allowed her to avoided parental punishment, but it allowed her guilt to fester. Unconsciously she flogged herself physically, mentally, emotionally, and spiritually, culminating with suicide.

The Inability to Admit You Are in the Wrong

I hate being wrong; however, considering I am a human being, it happens more often that I like, but that's just the way of life. The recognition of being wrong is the way I learn. Being wrong and admitting it by taking responsibility for inappropriate actions or words by way of an apology is never comfortable, but that is what adults do. Sadly, the flip side is separation.

Once I was in a situation with another person who did something to me that blatantly showed a lack of respect. Even though she had told me at one time I was her only real friend, her inability to apologize for her lack of respect was like cutting off her nose to spite her face. Without an apology informing me she was aware of her offensive behavior I had no assurance she wouldn't do it again. As a consequence, I refused to subject myself to further involvement with her. In the course of conversing with her about her refusal to apologize she told me she was blocked—an apt characterization of resistance.

Unlimited Opportunities

These examples cover just the possibilities I've observed, which may or may not apply to you because we are all different. Your veiled conflicts will be unique to you. Considering growth is an essential part of the definition of life, I believe our psyches continually place opportunities in our path to grow. Accepting that we have a problem is the first step in unlocking the prisons of conflict that dysfunctional beliefs put us in. Thankfully, we can do something about conflicts, veiled or not. Liberation is a choice, a choice to grow emotionally, and in the process, spiritually. While the idea of change may in itself feel threatening, living as you have been, immersed in fear-based threats as an everyday experience has got to be worse.

What have you got to lose by trying? While the experience of heaven on earth may seem the stuff of fairy tales, I assure you it is not. Emotional growth cannot eliminate all conflicts. Each day presents new issues that will need to be resolved. Using the exercises to resolve them eliminates the unconscious factor currently attaching you to your childhood fears. Once the veil of unconscious fear can no longer affect your perceptions, the existence of heaven on earth becomes self-evident.

Thoughts to Ponder

♦ Can you relate to any of the examples mentioned in this chapter?

♦ If Christ, Buddha, or Mohammed came and asked you to follow him today, could you do it? If not, what is standing in your way?

Part IV

Spiritual Liberation

Chapter 13

_____

Human Beings

When my journey began, the idea that my spiritual growth might be impaired had never occurred to me. After all, I'd been a faithful Episcopalian all my life. In retrospect, I think my assumption came from the belief that religions exist to stimulate spiritual growth. Like most assumptions, however, this one needs to be questioned.

Awareness of the distinction between our physical and spiritual bodies and the different forces that affect each body clarifies the issue.

The Basic Recipe

If you grant that God created human beings in his image, a recipe for assembling one of his children might read something like: combine one part physical body with one part spiritual body. As my experiences have demonstrated, these are *two manifestly different bodies,* each sustained by an *energy that is the direct opposite* of the other. Fear, conscious or unconscious, maintains the physical body, while God's unconditional love sustains the spiritual body. This distinction is the crux of the form of spiritual growth I am proposing.

Growth Part I: The Physical Body – Spirit's Vessel

During the first twelve to fifteen years of life, the natural focus of human growth is the physical body, which is in essence, spirit's vessel. Even though physical growth happens so slowly as to be imperceptible, its effects are obvious. When your feet outgrow your shoes, they begin pinching your toes, after a growth spurt, often boys begin ragging one another about wearing high waters, and one day, lo and behold, you find yourself looking down at your mother! Should growth seem impaired, parents take note and seek a doctor's advice.

During these formative years, unconscious fear is busily supporting the acquisition of the beliefs and social skills necessary for admittance to the familial order of the human race. Once this healthy, socially acceptable human being is established, the time comes to shift focus to developing the other, equally important component of who we are as human beings—the spiritual body.

Growth Part II: The Spiritual Body

As I define it, spiritual growth is a matter of expanding your ability to love, not as humans understand love, but as spirit loves. It occurs by eliminating the unconscious effects of fear so that you can experience your spiritual body.

Unlike physical growth, spiritual growth does not happen automatically, or is it inevitable. The very imperfection that allows us to function as human beings, fear, prevents our spiritual bodies from naturally evolving.

The fact that most coming-of-age initiations such as vision quests, bar and bat mitzvahs, as well as Christian confirmations occur during the early teenage years suggests that people around the world have, for centuries, recognized this period as the optimal time for spiritual growth. During this time, based on my experience minds are at their height of flexibility and open to new ideas. My interest in spiritual matters soared during this time. Like many teenagers, I sought sources of spiritual information, from the Bible to such outlandish things as Ouija boards and tarot cards. This heightened curiosity about all things related to spirit occurred not only to me but to my children and their teenage friends.

This consistency suggests human beings have internal clocks set to awaken us when our minds are ripe for spiritual growth. Even a formal introduction to mythology during this formative period would give young adults a broader foundation, a perspective that might prove invaluable later on when faced with the vagaries of life, the catastrophes that invariably occur.

Encouraging our natural predisposition to grow spiritually would allow us to formulate our own perception of life, as opposed to continuing to rely on our elders' opinions. Currently, a number of influences stifle curiosity in spiritual matters, from rigid religious dogmas and in some cases the popularity of organized sports programs or overzealous efforts to be admitted to the "right" college.

Without a spiritual connection, we have only the artifacts of the material world to give us security. Knowing that fear provides the basis of this security and that it exists only as long as we are in human form, as mentioned before anything rooted in the physical world can never assure security. The result is an unhealthy dependence on artifacts that the material world offers, like money.

Conflict – The Pinched Toes of Thwarted Growth

Thwarted spiritual growth has its version of pinched toes. These appear in the form of conflict. Some conflicts are obvious, but most show up under the guise of culturally accepted umbrellas like "should"—actions we are expected to take despite the distress they produce. One of my uncles never missed a chance to twist my ear. I despised having to go near the man. But because he was family, I had to attend events that included him. Every encounter with him was painful, yet when I thought about the suffering that he caused, it never occurred to me to refuse to attend a family event—it was one of those 'shoulds' membership in the family demanded.

The psychological roots of conflict are rarely identified and treated unless their expressions are blatant, such as when a student attempts to gun down classmates or when conflict creates so much stress that it causes heart problems or high cholesterol. As the all-important "they" are so fond of saying, these things are just how life is. Being the driving force of the human condition for so long, conflicts indicative of thwarted emotional and, therefore, spiritual growth have earned an undeserved level of acceptance.

The omnipresence of suffering and our mindless acceptance of it has led to the assumption that suffering is a natural part of life. To a certain degree it is and for some people it will always be. The suffering that such activities as war and abuse create is obvious, but nuanced conflicts are rarely if ever noticed and considered aberrant. Most conflicts indicate thwarted spiritual growth regardless of their severity.

While investigating spiritual resources, I attended a workshop in which I was led through a deep meditation. I was asked to envision stepping out of my identity and walking away. As I followed the instructions, a powerful, confident warrior appeared in my stead, totally foreign to anything I had ever recognized. Once the meditation ended, I walked by a mirror and glanced in it. The image I saw reflected was not the familiar face I expected to see but the powerful stranger who had appeared during the meditation. As my gaze lingered, I felt the muscles in my body swell with power and energy beyond anything I had ever known. Then it dawned on me. This magnificent, courageous warrior I saw reflected back to me was my true self—the one stripped of my current personality. The moment I realized this, my fear-generated identity snapped back and the present-day version of who I am, the distorted version based on my childhood beliefs, resumed control.

During my Pivotal Event, a similar experience occurred when I shed my prejudice. Inadvertently, the shedding erased the outgrown fear that had been unconsciously supporting the prejudice. When the prejudice vanished, the operational aspect of fear that had been sustaining it evaporated. A belief grounded in love immediately appeared and replaced the fear-based belief. Straightaway, a clear, unadulterated awareness of my spirit materialized—no fear, belief, resistance, emotion— nothing left to blind me to the perception of my spirit.

Invisible Glasses

Based on these experiences, it seems every day human beings awake wearing a pair of invisible glasses. Unlike sunglasses, the tint of these glasses comes from a thin film covering the lenses. The film is comprised of the fears our childhood beliefs generated. The film affects our perceptions 24/7 by blocking out anything incompatible with our primer's beliefs. This limitation preserves how we see ourselves and the world around us. Consequently, our understanding of experiences and the way we interpret them always comply with our unique version of reality; the one our childhood beliefs established.

Have you ever been astounded to hear someone else's opinion of you that is radically different from your own? How could this be, you ask? Other people are simply viewing you through their glasses, not through yours.

When I look in a mirror, my invisible glasses, allow me to see only the tainted version of who I *believe* I am, the "self" based largely on other people's opinions of me. This is not my true self. My beliefs mask my true identity. This brings into question who exactly is my authentic self. The image I first saw in the mirror after the meditation ended, the one stripped of my physical body's beliefs—my current identity as defined by my family's opinions of me.

I still need the human version of my identity in order to keep interacting with other people. On the other hand, my human version needs the influence that my spiritual body offers so that I can reach my potential as a human being. Ultimately, my potential is a matter of balance—my spiritual body developed to the extent it equals my human side.

Conditioned Obstructions

Years ago, behavioral psychologists[10] made a discovery that suggests how our invisible glasses come into being. The focus of their experiment was actually the vision of a litter of newborn kittens. Nevertheless, their discovery aptly illustrates not only the way our glasses originate, but the issues our glasses pose.

Shortly after birth, psychologists placed a litter of kittens in an environment that contained only horizontal features, such as flat objects. After an undetermined amount of time, the psychologists transferred the kittens to a typical environment, one that contained both horizontal and vertical objects. So, instead of seeing just the top of a table, they now saw a table with legs. The kittens immediately began crashing into vertical objects such as the legs of a table. Why? Their original environment conditioned the kittens to recognize only horizontal objects. Their *initial conditioning* rendered the kittens incapable of seeing the vertical objects in their new environment.

The reality that life introduces us to as we grow up is as one-sided as the one the kittens initially knew. This conditioning, like the kittens', allows us to perceive only a partial version of reality. Our brains cannot register or identify anything we were not initially conditioned to see or, as it were, believe. This matter is recognized as confirmation bias.

The parameters our conditioning establishes limit our perceptions in one of two ways. They either block alien information or alter it enough to make it acceptable (think fear-based) so that it verifies our reality. Therefore, what we end up believing always complies with the reality our conditioning initiated. Therefore, our concept of reality, like the one the kittens initially knew, is incomplete. Considering that fear initiated our perceptions of reality, we are not capable of recognizing anything that is not fear-based—in particular, our inherent spiritual bodies.

Once this problem dawned on me, I understood the difficulty I initially had with the five words from my dream: love is all that exists. Blinded by my conditioning, I could not accept such a radically alien concept. It made no sense whatsoever.

A Critical Realization

The experiment involving the kittens led to a critical revelation, fear obstructs our ability to perceive spirit. My Pivotal Event reinforced this observation. When acceptance of my greedy nature replaced my prejudice, fear supporting that belief vanished and in that moment awareness of spirit instantaneously pierced my heart. It was as if by removing a bit of the film covering the lenses of my "glasses," spirit was able to shine through.

Our glasses not only distort how we see ourselves, they automatically blind us to the alien nature of spirit. Our current, fear-based interpretation of spiritual subjects such as those reported in the Bible has corrupted our understanding of spirit.

Only concepts involving in fear, like anger, blame, or shame, are recognized in this reality. And vice versa; anything fear-based cannot appear in spirit's world as love is the opposite of fear.

Emotional growth eliminates the operational aspect of fear. The process removes the film covering our glasses. Thus, the prerequisite to spiritual growth is the type of emotional growth the exercises in Chapter 11 address.

Prisoners of the Human Condition

If human beings had our way, we would be sprawled out on lounge chairs alongside Adam and Eve waiting for our next meal to be served. The challenges of growing up have been daunting since the beginning of humanity. While there is a natural reluctance to sever the apron strings to our blood parents, severing the apron strings to what could be thought of as our psychological parent, unconscious fear, is close to impossible.

Resistance reigns. Even if emotional growth was recognized and encouraged, without rendering fear a mere awareness by way of the exercises, operational fear will continue overriding rational thought. We would rather snuggle deeper into our familiar, cozy nooks and commiserate with our fellow victims about such things as the price of oil, body fat, or finances rather than disturb the status quo. As such life seems satisfactory enough. Endless excuses support apathy, some convincing enough to further inaction, all due to the work of our psychological parent—operational fear.

For this reason, despite significant advances in technology, human beings remain emotional adolescents, prisoners of the illusion known as the human condition. We can't help ourselves. Sniff—we're victims. In much the same way as the idea that bad things happen when people do nothing, maintaining our current state of life only ensures that dissatisfaction will remain the rule of thumb.

Suffering, assumed to be the product of the human condition, *is not pre-ordained.* The choices we make determine the course of our lives. Engaging in emotional growth can feel intimidating because it involves change. Without the emotional growth required for the type of spiritual growth I am proposing, disaster lurks where least expected. However, the changes that this form of growth delivers transform the very beliefs that cause the suffering implicit in the human condition.

Handcuffed

Many beliefs will be necessary to retain throughout life, but not all. Some beliefs just are. Throw them out or not, it makes no difference. But when we find ourselves caught up in a you're-wrong-I'm-right quarrel, or stuck in a pit of staunch righteousness, we need to know the belief we are defending is not a casual, throw-it-out-or-not belief. Because this belief is causing conflict, it is probably safe to say it's dysfunctional; a belief that's been held past its "use-by" date. As long we remain clueless about the way fear unconsciously functions, ignorance will keep emotional/spiritual growth in irons. By eliminating the detrimental, dysfunctional beliefs that keep us imprisoned in emotional adolescence, we, and not our fears, can determine our lives. For this reason, it behooves us to rid ourselves of our dysfunctional crutches—our outgrown beliefs and fears.

By ignoring dysfunctional crutches, ridiculous situations such as the following occur. This situation arose because Jesse, Ken's father, was an only child when male progeny reigned supreme. On a hot summer morning when she went shopping, Sudi, Ken's grandmother, left her son, Jesse, in the yard with the houseman. During her absence, her sister-in-law walked past Sudi's house en route to the swimming hole with her son. Seeing her nephew alone in the yard, she invited Jesse to join them. After getting permission from the houseman, Jesse's aunt left with the two boys happily in tow.

When Sudi returned and discovered her sister-in-law had taken her son swimming without her permission, she was livid. Even though Jesse returned unharmed, Sudi refused to speak to her sister-in-law again. For over thirty years, these two women lived in that small Appalachian town of less than a thousand people and never spoke to one another again. Had Sudi's self-righteousness indignation not been so gratifying, I suspect her attachment to her anger might have diminished. But this fear-based attachment kept stoking her fires of justification, reinforcing the wall her mind erected around the incident.

The relationship we have with our beliefs and the security we unconsciously assume they offer make us human. However, when we outgrow a belief or develop an unhealthy dependence on one, it can be the most potent impediment to change. Until the Pivotal Event, it never occurred to me to question my family's prejudice against my father's sisters. Even when I was forty years old, the infantile fear of losing my parent's love kept my emotional growth in irons.

The possibility that human beings can control behaviors once considered immutable raises the prospect of a future never thought possible. In the past, only a fool dared believe that humans could exist without conflicts that produce war. Even though conflicts are inevitable, we need to experience them. They are the means by which we learn how to become better human beings. However, the inevitability of conflict does not cancel out the possibility of peace. Peace could reign if enough people rendered their fears as simple awarenesses by unearthing and eliminating their operational aspect. Then war could become a thing of the past. All it takes is emotional growth.

The Human Concept of Love

As long as we rely on our fear-based beliefs, they determine who and what we can accept and love. In this case, the ability to love, or even accept another person or thing, requires that that person or thing accords with our beliefs. This requirement is the definition of conditional love.

The Theory of Everything is a film about Steven Hawking's life. It covers his life before and after his illness and ends with the last stages of his life. The turning point occurs when his wife, who has been his sole caregiver, becomes fed up with her role as his caregiver. Wife, yes, but Steven is no longer the man he was when first they married. This realization proves to be too painful for her. She hires a nurse to take care of him. To his wife's amazement, the nurse and Steven develop a loving relationship. How can this be, you might ask? The nurse had just signed up to be his caregiver and had no previous knowledge of Steven. Unlike his wife, the nurse's lack of expectation freed her to appreciate who Steven was at the time they met. Without his wife's knowledge of who he had been, the nurse could love Steven as he was then.

There is always something beautiful within each of us to cherish if, and only if, we can overcome beliefs that dictate who and how we love. Diseases change people. Losing the version of a person we first fell in love with often hinders our ability to keep loving them. This I well know, as my husband's dementia kept changing him. However, even as our loved ones change, underneath their outward presentations, there still exists that beautiful, loveable human being we fell in love with, one perhaps more capable of reciprocating the love we show them because they no longer have the demands of work to distract them.

There is a Cherokee tale in which a grandfather tells his grandson about two wolves living within us. One represents our negative tendencies, the other our positive ones. The grandfather tells his grandson these wolves are constantly fighting one another. When the boy asks which wolf will win, the grandfather says, "The wolf you feed."

The previous chapters have focused on the anatomy of the wolf that fear feeds—our human side. The following chapters depict, for lack of a better word, the wolf that love, or that spirit feeds.

Thoughts to Ponder

♦ Think of a scenario in which you reacted emotionally with disastrous results. Now, try imagining how being aware and in control of your fear might have affected the outcome.

♦ Some religions focus on denigrating our physical bodies, however, without a physical body, how could our spiritual bodies function?

Chapter 14

Your Potential Power

There may be many ways to reach our potential as human beings. The one I am proposing requires a type of emotional growth that removes part of the film covering your invisible glasses. As growth ensues, our spiritual bodies become increasingly apparent. As this perception expands, a relationship with our spiritual selves develops. In equal measure, as our relationship with our spiritual connection expands, we function with the level of power of which we are capable. Trust in our spiritual connection allows us to reach our potential as human beings.

The nature of our potential power differs from the usual idea of power which is power *over* someone or something. Power over is a divisive form of power and often results in winners and losers. The power that spiritual growth produces is more about reciprocal healing, building community—in short, compassionate motivation. It can have surprising results.

An Example of Traditional Power

The story of *The Three Little Pigs* is familiar to most people who grew up in America. According to my 1948 book version of the fable, adapted from the Walt Disney motion picture of the same name, three little pigs, who are brothers, set out to build their homes. The first two brothers preferred dancing, singing, and following their whims rather than working. The first brother builds his house of straw and the second brother builds his house of sticks. Once accomplished, the two set out to see how their other brother is getting along. Seeing him toiling away, building his house of bricks, they make fun of him. He couldn't have cared less. He chastised his brothers, telling them he will be safe and they will be sorry when the wolf comes to their doors. They pay him no heed. Laughing at their brother's warning, the two brothers dance away to their houses only to face the wolf.

When the wolf blows down the houses of the first two brothers, they seek refuge in their brother's house of brick. Unable to blow down this house, the wolf contrives an alternate plan and goes down the chimney. When he does, he lands in a cauldron of boiling water. With a yelp of pain, he springs back up the chimney, never to be seen again.

Real-life Example of Traditional Power

By continuing to rely on childhood beliefs, disaster lurks where least expected. While giving workshops in churches on the psychological pathway I had developed for spiritual growth, I came across a situation that exemplified this problem. I had begun giving workshops on spiritual growth using the exercises in this book. Considering spiritual growth was the goal, I assumed the greatest interest in my workshop would be in churches.

Finding audiences was a painful and lengthy process. It began by sending a letter of introduction and a brochure describing my workshop to a church. Later, I would follow this up with a cold call, more letters, more calls, and, if I was lucky, an interview with the head of education or, if the congregation was small, the church minister.

So, in keeping with my process, I sent my letter of introduction and brochure to the minister of a popular church in the area. Ten days later, I made the usual follow-up cold call. To my utter astonishment, the minister's secretary told me he wanted to see me *that* morning. The immediacy of this invitation should have alerted me to the fact something was amiss, but it didn't.

Blinded by enthusiasm, I pounced on the offer. Due to the many positive responses I had received earlier, the implications of the title of my workshop, "Inner Peace, Outer Love" (which I now am embarrassed to admit), had never crossed my mind. Given what transpired that day though, I strongly suspect the title was the reason this minister jumped at the chance to lure me in.

In 1990, the hippie flower-child stigma from the 1970s still lingered. At the same time, men's attitudes towards women remained Victorian. At best, women were considered inferior, ditzy beings never to be taken seriously. So, there I was a woman who wanted to convince a man to allow me to present an oddball, airy-fairy workshop to his respectable congregation. The combination proved irresistible. The minister couldn't let it pass. Long before I entered his office, I suspect the man had assumed he knew who I was and was eager to challenge me.

I had barely entered his office before the man began verbally attacking me. At first, I thought he was trying to be funny in a perverted sort of way. but when his comments became caustic, it was evident humor was the last thing on his mind. It seemed he was determined to expose me as just another featherbrained woman.

Peacocking his superiority, he launched his attempt to strip me of my pretensions. It quickly became apparent if I had any hope of leaving the man's office without being flogged, it was up to me to keep the conversation on a dignified, positive level. Concentrating everything I had on what the man was saying, I was able to distill something I could constructively respond to. For what seemed an eternity, the man badgered me with insults and insinuations that were neither clever nor original. I imagine records of the Salem witch trials contain much the same material.

Eliciting hysterical responses from me was exactly what the man wanted. Even the slightest hint of emotion or reaction from me would have corroborated his assumptions, supplying him with the ammunition he needed to continue needling me. Being aware of what the minister was doing allowed me to separate myself from the verbal garbage he kept pelting me with. Keeping a gaggle of two-year-olds from destroying a house would probably have been easier.

Despite the extremes the minister went to goad me, I never responded as he expected. I never lashed out, lost control, or began sobbing uncontrollably. My ability to stay the course deprived the man of any incentive to keep up his assault. Robbed of the responses I suspect he was hoping to elicit, the minister was at a loss. After about forty-five minutes of grilling, it became apparent he was losing steam. Faltering, he ended the conversation by saying, "Well, Mrs. Tuggle, I just want you to know, you pass muster." In other words, I didn't fall apart under his interrogation.

This comment stunned me so much it didn't matter that I didn't get the job. It was the biggest win I could have hoped for, given the circumstances. I may have convinced the minister of the merit of my workshop by not falling apart, but as I think about it, exposing myself more by giving my workshop in the man's church was the last thing I would have wanted to do, even if he had given me the opportunity

Once a child reaches seven years old or thereabouts, most parents lose their ability to control their child. When this happens, to establish superiority, parents commonly resort to threats or use outside forces to maintain control of their child. The child in turn, mimics these behaviors to empower themselves—likely the seed I suspect, that leds to bullying. Without exposure to alternative ways of behaving, adults, like the minister, perpetuate these antiquated, fear-based forms of power. Even now, at moments when I lack awareness, I am ashamed to admit, I have found myself engaging in an antiquated type of power. This may have been the case with the minister, whose behavior reflected puerile beliefs.

The Wolf Walks—An Example of Love-Based Power

As long as we keep our security blankies (fear-generated beliefs) clutched tightly to our chest, there will always be a big bad wolf lurking somewhere, waiting for just the right moment to trip us up and rip our blankies from the grasp of our sticky little fingers. When it's not an actual wolf at the door but something on the order of a dramatic downward trend in the stock market, security alarms peal. "The wolf's at the door, the wolf's at the door!" And like the fabled three pigs, we panic. With only the thought of safety in mind, we run. With the wolf (fear) in hot pursuit, we sprint along the three little pigs' rutted path and sell off our stocks. The problem is that other stockholders' emotions have energized them too. And like us, they are doing the piggy thing. Havoc spirals. Chaos rules. The stock market crashes, an altogether nasty business!

The pigs' fight-or-flight path is no longer the only option for dealing with threats. Naysayers contend these behaviors are automatic, so deeply embedded in our psyches that it is impossible to disengage from them. While that may have been true once, it no longer necessarily is. Fight-or-flight impulses will never disappear, nor should they, especially for children. After all, these impulses have ensured human survival for eons.

For adults, continued obedience to these impulses can be highly detrimental. In this technological age where one mindless act can obliterate our earth and all life force on it, obeying our emotional impulses can be cataclysmic. Fortunately, as my revised version of "The Three Little Pigs" will show, an alternate to fight-or-flight impulses exists, the consequences of which are positive. Awareness is the key. With awareness, adults can disengage themselves from emotions that fear generates—the cause of detrimental behaviors. With emotions in check, a revised version of this story might go something like this.

All the pigs in this rendering of their story read my book several years ago. Since then, they have been diligently working through the exercise. Now, having rendered fear inoperable numerous times by dying to themselves, or in other words, their outgrown, fear-generated beliefs, they find themselves increasingly able to function with awareness. So, on a day when the big bad wolf starts huffing and puffing outside their house *again* (would you believe the old coot is still up to such antics?), instead of hysterically responding as they did in the past, clutching their blankies for all their worth and dashing out of their houses to escape the monster, my enlightened porcine troupe gather to discuss their options. Before, when emotions ran rampant, this was not possible, but the brothers are now in control of themselves, their emotions, and their actions.

So now, upon hearing the wolf thundering around their yard *again,* bellowing his tired old threats, a peculiar new idea occurs to the members of my troupe. Maybe the wolf is terrorizing them because the poor thing's just hungry. A full belly is all he wants! With the wolf bellowing at the top of his lungs in their front yard, a new plan occurs to my troupe. One of the pigs remembers the roast sitting on the shelf in their fridge, which they had planned to have for Sunday dinner. The three brothers gleefully run to the kitchen, grab the roast and toss it out the back door. Upon hearing the kitchen door slam, the beast dashes around the house, spots the meat, and bolts it down in one gargantuan gulp. After giving a resounding burp, the wolf, now satiated, trots off into the woods, curious to see what Little Red Riding Hood might be up to.

For a story whose traditional ending involved violence and hostility, this alternative resolution is altogether positive. Before, under the influence of fear, the pigs' choices were limited—run or kill the wolf. These fight-or-flight choices rarely, if ever, produce favorable resolutions for everyone involved, someone always loses. Even though my version is a work of fiction, its resolution is totally feasible. By releasing the brain from the clutches of emotions that unconscious fear generates, positive, creative alternatives never before imagined can and do become possible.

Win-Win Power

Love-based power is perhaps more potent, more formidable than the time-honored power detailed in my story about the minister. Suffering is never involved, no one loses at the cost of another person's gain. Instead, it creates win-win situations. For example, the minister's initial approach violated everything Christ taught about "Judge not, that ye be not judged" (Matthew 7:1). The win-win approach of my conversation with him prevented the minister from further diminishing himself as a Christian leader. And yes, while I wasn't hired to give workshops at his church, having my behavior gain his approval was a decided win for me.

The ultimate goal of this book is to encourage a form of spiritual growth, which has been pointed out, is the result from a particular practice of emotional development. This method creates awareness. Awareness is power, awareness offers control, the type of control in which we, not operational fear, govern our emotions, thoughts, and actions. Awareness gives us the presence of mind to neutralize threatening situations before fear foments chaos. The results can be profound.

A few years ago, I heard a woman tell a story that illustrates the positive effects created by the type of awareness that allows us to govern our emotions. According to what she told me, the woman suddenly found herself accosted by a man intending to rape her. In the face of the attack, the woman surprised herself by reacting uncharacteristically. Instead of trying to fight him off or scream for help, she found herself saying to the man, "I forgive you." This response stupefied the man. Immediately, he began shaking with sobs. At this point, he and the woman found a bench to sit on and started talking. It turns out the man had just lost his job. Being jobless demoralized him but was hurting his family, too. Knowing this, it became apparent to the woman that any "normal" reaction when he initially approached her would have heightened his sense of disgrace and sent him spiraling further out of control. Thankfully, due to the woman's awareness and ability to control her emotions, that didn't happen.

I want to think most of the time I can maintain a balanced focus even in the most challenging situations. The truth is, I am successful only half the time. However, when I am aware and on my toes, the ability to adjust what I say and do can resolve problems in the most remarkable ways. Regarding my interview with the minister, I only survived his interrogation as well as I did because I had achieved a modicum of awareness. I knew I needed to approach him from a place of love. Had I approached the man in my youth when I was fear-centered and emotionally driven, I hate to think how things might have turned out. Based on my childhood experiences I would have automatically assumed the man's acidic comments were about me—a defamation of my character.

That day, this idea never occurred to me. Since we'd only just met, it seemed apparent his remarks had nothing to do with me and everything to do with him. It was about his fears and beliefs. Had I been as lacking in emotional maturity as he was, we surely would have come to fisticuffs, with me slinking off with my tail between my legs. In short, awareness allowed me to remain objective, without judgment, and therefore, proactive. Awareness allowed me to *choose* the most positive path. Everyone profited.

Under the influence of operational fear, awareness is nearly impossible. Conflicts led us to think our lives (beliefs) are at stake. By using the indirect "back door" approach of the exercises we render operational fear impotent. Awareness results.

Thoughts to Ponder

◆ In the past, what did reaching your potential mean to you?

◆ How might the revised version of *The Three Little Pigs* affect your thoughts about power?

◆ Most people give lip-service to wanting peace on earth. Which form of power do you think would make peace on earth a real possibility?

Chapter 15

For Only One Season

When a butterfly caterpillar encases itself in a chrysalis, it submits its body to chaos and the disintegration required to emerge as a new being. Emerging as a butterfly can only happen if the caterpillar's body completely breaks down. If only human beings could allow our beliefs, those transient nurturers that guide us through the choppy waters of infancy, to fall away when their season is past. Then, like a caterpillar, a being as awe-inspiring as a butterfly could emerge. If only…

Metaphorically, the beliefs in our primer for Life 101 creates our chrysalises. Operational fear works to preserve that chrysalis. The ways in which operational fear preserves our primer prevents the processes of transformation, natural to caterpillars, from occurring. The need to preserve our childhood beliefs encases us in our chrysalises. The natural process of deterioration sets in. In this wasted state, people resist the change that growth portends—all because of the unconscious association of beliefs with being our existence and the security we unconsciously associate with them. For us to emerge as the equivalent of a butterfly, outgrown beliefs that encase us need to disintegrate.

Absent the natural cycle of disintegration and transformation, "the human condition" will continue following the same torturous path it's been on since it began. Lest you think knowing this might encourage people to welcome change—if not for ourselves, then for creating a more peaceful future for our children—you will be disappointed. Tragically, due to our unconscious disposition, the unrecognized relationship we have with our beliefs disallows our ability to accept radical ideas that change portends. As stated earlier, the imprisoning supposition is—*if I lose a belief, my physical body dies.* In other words, the loss of a belief will extinguish my life because my psyche treats my beliefs as if they are my actual life.

The Benefits of Disintegrating: Emotional Growth

For the time it takes us to develop the ability to fend for ourselves as children, we need operational fear protecting us. After we reach adulthood, we are in a position to take responsibility for ourselves. Theoretically, we no longer need fear parenting us, but unless we bring the operational aspect to light, it will continue. The continued parenting of fear compels us to cling to the very elements that prevent emancipation. Shackled by unconscious forces, our brains automatically stifle true spiritual growth. The forces supporting this impediment are an illusion. Because it is so deeply ingrained, overcoming our dependency on this illusion is nearly impossible. Life is out of sync when operational fear continues controlling our thoughts and actions. Dependency on these parents prolongs disharmony, suffering, and stress from the conflicts it causes that often leads to disease.

When I was growing up, laptops and cell phones were nonexistent. Typewriters and landline phones ruled communications until I was about forty years old. It could be said my welfare depended on the use of typewriter and telephones. Once computers replaced typewriters and cell phones replaced landline phones, had my ability to communicate continued relying on these older technologies, this dependency would have created a disconnect. Conflict would have been inevitable.

In the same way that the newer ways of communicating far outweigh the benefits that typewriters and telephones offer, childhood beliefs are no match for the knowledge, strength, and wisdom gained through emotional growth. The older you are, the better equipped you are to handle the disruption that transforming outdated beliefs creates.

Christmas was a week away when my son, Edward, then age ten, began asking me *again* about Santa Claus. Was Santa Claus really real? His question put me in a dither. I, who had spent hours listening to Bruno Bettelheim encouraging parents to allow their young children to believe in anything, tooth fairies, invisible friends, gnomes, and Santa Claus, couldn't decide what to say to my son. Should I tell him now or let his friends ridicule him because he still believed in Santa? Finally, I decided. I would gently introduce Edward to the idea that Santa Claus was the spirit of Christmas, not an actual person. After listening to my loving explanation, Ed went to his room. A short while later he returned and announced, "This has been the worst day of my life."

The news that Santa Claus is not a real person shook Edward's world to the core; nevertheless, it didn't destroy him. Despite still being a vulnerable ten-year-old boy, Edward had the love and support of his family to turn to for help. Our love helped him emotionally rebalance himself, which kept him on an even keel as his belief in Santa Claus imploded.

The Illusion

When a body dies, the beliefs that that body's mind embraced die along with it. Considering that beliefs are only artifacts of our human bodies, the fact is they are as immaterial and imaginary as the emperor's new clothes. Therefore, whether by decree, choice, or death, those crucial, transitory features that fear has unconsciously convinced us are prerequisites for our ability to exist, the beliefs that comprise our chrysalises, can and do vanish.

As Vatican II's decision about eating meat on Fridays illustrates, beliefs are a work of fiction—an illusion. For centuries mystics have been claiming the same thing— life is an illusion. Emotional growth can bring us to the same conclusion. Personally, I don't think of myself as being a mystic. This is probably due to an outdated idea of who a mystic is and how they present themselves in life. Regardless, if the recognition that life is an illusion is a concept that only mystics understand, then well, I suppose I am a mystic.

Adam and Eve's Illusion

Returning to Adam and Eve's expulsion from Eden, the *only real change* that Adam and Eve experienced happened to their perceptions—the way they perceived life and the world around them. Everything else about their circumstances remained as it had been from the beginning. However, because fear unconsciously began affecting their perceptions, their beliefs about their circumstances radically changed. The changes they allegedly reported were, as I have come to believe, figments of their newly affected perceptions and, therefore, an illusion.

Their new sense of alienation or separation (the definition of sin) exemplifies the fact that their perceptions have switched. The reality they now perceive, a dichotomy of separation as opposed to their former awareness of unity, reflects how fear unconsciously has begun affecting their brains. Their transformed perceptions affect everything about their lives, especially the relationship they have with their father.

When their minds knew only love, judgment that operational fear generates never occurs to them. But no longer. Once they become oblivious to their former relationship with God and their spirit selves, dichotomy rules their perceptions. The lens through which they now view the world separates everything they come across as being either right, wrong, good, bad, or evil. Thus, they've become incarcerated in an illusion of beliefs that form their chrysalis.

The Disintegration of My Chrysalis

As a child, by adopting the family prejudice I became an acceptable member of my family. In terms of caterpillars, this belief became part of my body as a caterpillar. Once it became dysfunctional—separating me from my greater family, the belief and all that solidified it constituted my chrysalis. The purpose of this stage is metamorphosis for both a caterpillar and for human beings. For a caterpillar, it is the death of its body.

For human beings, it is also the death of our bodies, but not our actual selves. It is the death of a belief that operational fear equates as being us. In my case, this metamorphosis occurred when the operational aspect of fear responsible for safeguarding my belief (prejudice) evaporated, or died as it were. The death of this body (belief) allowed me to emerge as a new being. Referring to my Pivotal Event, the new being that emerged was a metamorphosis of perception so extreme it was if I was not the same person I was before. In Christian terms, it could be thought of in terms of being born again. I was born anew. The resulting awareness that I was not only a human being, but also a spiritual being, was my equivalent of becoming a butterfly.

Dividing the Men From the Boys

Throughout my life, I have experienced several types of spiritual experiences. The first kind occurred during my baptism when I was four months old. The memory didn't take shape until as a teenager I returned to the church where I had been baptized. Sitting in the pew that day, I couldn't believe there wasn't a light fixture above the baptismal font. For some reason I was positive there would be a light above the font. The omission jogged my memory. It was then I fully recalled the experience. As the bishop performed the baptismal ritual, I clearly remember seeing white light streaked with blue and gold radiating above my head as love engulfed me.

My family continued to attend this church until I was three or four years old. Each time we went I recall insisting we sit as close to the baptismal font as possible. Mother claimed the reason for my insistence was because I wanted to see babies being baptized. Not at all. The truth is I longed to re-experience my baptism, which unbeknownst to me had continued haunting me. Spiritual experiences of this nature continued to occur. They appeared as forms of solace, much like a parent's loving embrace. All were singular events. Each one reminded me that Spirit, God, or the Universe, if you will, is always present, loving me.

The second type of spiritual experience was a different matter altogether. Compared to my former parent-child spiritual embraces, the results of with my Pivotal Event divided the men from the boys so to speak. A mature relationship with spirit resulted because it established *a conscious connection* with spirit. I say it was mature because it allowed me to interact and work with spirit. This awareness caused a change in my behavior. Even though the word, love, can be used a noun, when we say we love someone, love is a verb. Implicit in its use as a verb, love is expressed as an action. I feel discord when I am not behaving as my best, loving self. As a consequence, I choose to act in a more loving way. A change in behavior is the defining characteristic of the spiritual growth I am proposing. Consequently, love has begun replacing fear as the determining factor for my thoughts and behaviors.

By allowing my outgrown "self" to disintegrate, I am slowly emerging as the powerful human being I was created to be.

Thoughts to Ponder

♦ Where would you say you are in the process of becoming a butterfly (metaphorically speaking)?

♦ What are some reasons you might find spiritual growth difficult?

♦ Does knowing you are a spiritual being inhabiting a human body change your thoughts about either body?

♦ How does knowing your body serves as a vessel for your spirit affect how you treat your body?

Part V

The Pathway Back to Paradise

Chapter 16

Spiritual Growth

Before and After

T he instant Adam and Eve's awareness of fear turned operational, it began influencing their perceptions. The result was the muddled version of God that religion introduced me to that begins taking shape immediately after Adam and Eve answer God's question. This characterization of God is the one Hebrews, Muslims, and Christians first adopted and sadly still believe to be true.

Considering that fear is the antithesis of love, operational fear treats the love that spirit recognizes as a threat. To eliminate this peril, the brain reframes all references to God and spirit to reflect fear—to wit, the concept of sin, the devil, and the idea of an angry, punishing God. Consequently, our understanding of spiritual growth has been compromised. Now it is the product of fear, not love. This happens because our brains resist the level of interference required to engage our spiritual bodies.

As long as operational fear controls our thoughts, it fends off the perception of Paradise.

Most concepts involving spirit that currently exist are fear-based and, therefore, are distorted. The Old Testament portrayal of God in Genesis is probably the most egregious example. Here an ostensibly unconditionally loving God is portrayed as an angry father who judges. Echoes of this characterization appear throughout the Old Testament. This portrayal presents us with a problem. Only fear has the ability to foment anger considering that fear is the antithesis of love. If, as stated in 1 John 4:16, "God is love," in Spirit's reality, love alone exists. Logically therefore, any reference to a loving God who is capable of anger is a flagrant contradiction of terms. This warped concept of God resembles the myth of Santa Claus; naughty children get coal and good little boys and girls get gifts. This is the antithesis of unconditional love—which is, *love without any condition attached.*

In all probability, the Biblical authors whose portrayal of God we read from Genesis 3 on had never experienced unconditional love. The idea of a heavenly father who loves regardless of anything they do was a markedly alien concept, it stumped them. The only model of a father they had was their own—someone who determined good from bad and ruled accordingly. Not only that, everyone knew you had to please your father, abide by his rules, or suffer his wrath. How can you please a father who loves you regardless of who you are or what you do? What does this father punish you for? Such a foreign idea of God violated the very foundation of beliefs that their lives depended upon. A heavenly father who was just like their fathers—a God who determined good from bad, expressed anger, and leveled punishments, now that God was the type of father they could relate to.

For centuries, humans have created religions based on the lives of avatars (an incarnation of a deity on earth), and prophets like Moses, Mohamed, and Jesus Christ. Regardless of what a prophet may have *actually* said, how the human beings who heard their words *understood them* is a different matter altogether. Knowing what I do now, I believe their human brains couldn't help but influence the creeds they passed along. This is nowhere more apparent than the verses in the New Testament advocating separate treatment of women or people of a different color or race—a gross contradiction of Christ's greatest commandments about love (Matthew 22:37).

Muddled Concept of Love

Most people think they understand what it means to love unconditionally—total acceptance without any conditions attached. Based on our behavior though, we have missed the point. Until now, whether we realize it or not, our *beliefs determine* who or what we can or cannot love. The first time this issue came to my attention occurred when the son of my favorite aunt divorced his wife. Previously, I would have sworn this aunt was the one person I thought loved unconditionally; however, when faced with accepting her son's divorce, she was at a loss. According to her staunch Catholic beliefs, divorce was a sin. From the little I observed, her belief about her son's divorce seemed to create a rift in their relationship.

Love that begets separation is not unconditional.

Fear and unconditional love are diametric opposites, the yin and yang of each other. Because spirit's domain is the antithesis of fear, it is impossible for the emotions that fear generates, such as anger, to occur in spirit's domain. The reverse is true. In our reality, unconsciously founded on fear, the ability to perceive pure spirit does not readily happen. Pure spirit constitutes a threat to the basis of our reality. For this reason, we have significantly altered the concept of unconditional love. I suspect this is why Christ

179

taught in parables. This indirect method of teaching furnished Christ with the means to convey radical spiritual concepts to audiences whose minds were unconsciously controlled by fear. Tell them something that challenged their beliefs and Christ might have been written off as just another zealot—thrown out along with his alien, unconsciously threatening notions. Given the times and the circumstances he faced, the guy did his best.

Beliefs Vis à Vis Religion

Just as fear unconsciously limits individual beliefs, it also limits the information that religions can provide. The Christian religion I know actively works against the change that generates spiritual growth, as I define it. According to my early experiences as an Episcopalian, a religion's principal focus seems to be the preservation of its doctrines, which may be argued exist to inspire spiritual growth. However, the inescapable fact that fear is unconsciously entrenched in these doctrines, affects the type of spiritual growth a religion can encourage.

For close to fifty years, I attended weekly services at my family's Episcopal church. Once Ken and I moved to our farm, however, I stopped attending weekly services. Driving an hour on Sunday mornings to attend church was more than I was willing to do. During my absence, without knowing it, my spiritual growth blossomed.

Several years later, I return to this church. As I walked into the vestibule, it felt like I'd come home. The feeling was so powerful that I wondered why I had stayed away for so long. Singing the well-known hymns, going through the ritual, repeating prayers I knew by heart felt so good. As I was simmering in these time-honored traditions, a shocking idea suddenly pierced my serenity.

It *felt like I was being suffocated.* Suffocated? Later as I thought about this disturbing idea, a vexing idea dawned on me, the church is a womb from which there is no birth.

In retrospect, the idea had been developing in me for years. After forty years of absorbing the basic tenets of the church, the inherent contradictions and inconsistencies within the written word as well as what I was hearing interpreted in sermons began to dawn on me. I tried discussing these observations with my priest without much success. And so, they remained disturbing oddities. Then in the eighties, when environmental problems finally caught my attention, my spiritual insights about it collided smack dab into the impenetrable wall that the church's doctrine posed.

Considering the environment is God's creation, I felt the church needed to treat it more as a sacred entity than something that exists only to benefit human beings. The church needed to be more responsive to how it was contributing to environmental problems. We had a committee on human justice, so why, I wondered, didn't we have a committee on environmental justice? When I tried sharing these thoughts with our priest, he said he couldn't discuss such out-of-the-box (my words) ideas, they were beyond the church's purview. As a priest of the church, his job was to support the church's doctrines. He was, therefore, obliged to reject notions such as I was proposing because they conflicted with Christian doctrine. After finding a non-Christian label to stick on my suggestion, the conversation ended and that was that. Experiences like these gave rise to the shocking idea that came to me during that brief return, and because of them, the restrictive nature of doctrines and dogmas became apparent to me.

The essential nature of life is growth. Like a womb, religions offer abundant nourishment that stimulates a neophyte's growth. For growth to continue though, birth must occur not only for a fetus but, as unconventional an idea as it is, for religious neophytes too. However, the womb that doctrines form aborts a neophyte's ability to keep growing. The inflexibility of doctrines prevents growth that automatically comes with birth, in the form of expansion of ideas outside doctrine, because doctrines are fear-based. The inability to breach the wall that doctrines pose portends death. This may be the reason many mainline churches are losing congregants. Nevertheless, all beliefs serve as important springboards.

As Bruno Bettelheim reminded the group of mothers who met with him in Chicago on Saturday mornings, of which I was a member in 1969, even fairy tales, myths, and magical beings such as Santa Claus offer an essential foundation for a child's spiritual growth. According to him, without a basis to question, developing an adult belief system able to handle life's enigmas can be extremely difficult.

Horizontal Growth

After a body reaches its maximum height, growth continues on a cellular level. As to actual physical growth beyond this period, it becomes a matter of adding fat, sometimes muscle, but mainly fat. Expanding waistlines is a horizontal form of growth. Adding to your spirit-related knowledge of other people's experiences, interpretations, or insights, could be considered similarly—a horizontal form of growth. Reading about Thomas Merton's mystical experience of oneness while he stood on the corner of Fourth and Walnut in Louisville, Kentucky, is fuel for thought, but simply knowing about his mystical experience cannot recreate the remarkable event. [11] Any one can have an equivalent encounter, but only when unconscious fear no longer totally governs perceptions.

The limitations that doctrines impose restrict spiritual development. The result is a horizontal type of growth. Forty years of repeating the same prayers and hearing the same biblical passages read had little effect on how I behaved. Despite my desperate desire to change, my behavior remained unaffected. Doctrines perpetuate a horizontal mindset that squelches any attempt to grow spiritually beyond its doctrines. Horizontal growth limits our ability to expand our understanding of love, in particular unconditional love.

No wonder I was initially dumbfounded by my dream's message that all that exists is love. Still spellbound by the illusion of fear, my ability to understand, much less believe such a reality could exist as those five words suggest, violated my version of reality. My then fear-based brain considered such an idea the stuff of fairy tales.

Vertical Growth

Working through the exercises in this book begins eliminating parts of the film of fear covering the lenses of our invisible glasses—the film that governs our ability to perceive spirit. Each time I repeat the exercises, a clearer understanding of spirit comes to light.

This differs from horizontal growth in two significant ways. It frees spiritual concepts from the limitations of fear. Initially, who we were taught to believe we were determined how we behaved. Through emotional growth our transformed beliefs and the insights we gain significantly affect how we think and therefore, behave.

An adult relationship with spirit begins replacing the obedient child that doctrine would have us remain.

At least, that is how the communion prayer, once used in the Episcopal Church, made me feel. "We are not worthy so much as to gather up the crumbs under thy Table." [12] That prayer emphasized my worthlessness. It twisted my heart with humiliation. If I had to offer a positive defense of the prayer, it ensured no one dared think of themselves as God. The worthlessness this prayer emphasized left no question. I was and would always be a needy child, perpetually dependent on the church. Given this inferred status, how dare I attempt to grow up and think for myself? In this way, my religion not only limited my growth to the extent its doctrine allowed, but encouraged a type of childhood dependency.

Because the church reinforces traditional ways of thinking, especially through the concept of sin, followers continue to think of themselves as depraved children, obedient to an angry God. A feature in the Catholic church my mother grew up attending visually sums up the nature of this God. A massive mosaic of a single *blue* eye—the eye of God, hovers in the center of the cupola covering the nave of the church. Looking at that mosaic struck me as being so outrageous, the implications the blue eye suggested, that a *Caucasian* God is watching every move you make was so ridiculous it unnerved me to the extent I didn't know whether to vomit or laugh.

Changed Behavior Indicates Vertical Growth

The adult relationship with spirit that vertical growth generates has *significantly expanded my perspective.* Increasingly, love determines my thoughts and behaviors.

While the idea of releasing traditional doctrines might seem intimidating, like jumping off a cliff into the unknown, consider this. Ideas advanced by Einstein did not diminish or disprove Newton's theories, they expanded them. In the same way, vertical spiritual growth does not diminish the teachings of an avatar. For Christians, I have found that the insights from vertical growth flesh out and enliven Christ's message of love and give meaning to his sometimes-confusing parables. Most importantly, this expanded perspective reveals ways to turn love into the verb it is.

The most valuable aspect of vertical growth is the ability to recognize the innate aspect each of us shares: *spirit*. This awareness unites all human beings, regardless of race, creed, or sexual orientation, *as one being, made in the image of God.* At this point, *what I am*, spirit currently contained within a human body, becomes more important than *who I am,* the sum of the beliefs that comprise my identity. This significantly changes how I think and more importantly, how I behave—a characteristic that indicates actual spiritual growth.

With vertical growth, inconceivable ideas come to light, like one I mentioned earlier from Father Greg Boyle referring to "the whateverness of God." As nonconformist a concept as it is, the reference captures the essence of vertical growth.

Two Cans of Paint

Unbeknownst to us, fear unconsciously taints our perceptions of Spirit rendering them horizontal concepts. Whereas vertical perceptions are untainted. To give you an idea of how our present horizontal understanding of spirit is tainted I offer the following illustration. Imagine you see before you two cans of paint. One can represents fear and the other love *as spirit expresses it.* For the sake of argument, let's say the color of the paint in the can representing fear is green and the color of the paint in the can representing spirit is red.

One day, while immersed in your lovely green world, you decide you want to investigate Spirit's red world because you would like to experience it. So, you go to the paint store and ask the clerk to add red colorant to your can of already brimming with green paint. The clerk takes your can to his workroom and stirs in red colorant. Having never come into contact with pure red, you assume the color of the paint in your can is now pure red.

The fact is, it is not pure red, nor can it ever be. Regardless of how much red colorant you add to your can, the *original color will always affect the resulting color.* The end product will be a shade of taupe, or an off-shade of red depending on how much colorant has been added. It will never be pure red. However, because you have never seen pure red, you are unable to recognize the paint in your can is an altered version of red.

And that's the problem. It is impossible for fear-based mindsets to understand, much less encourage vertical growth. Regardless of being inspired by God, human beings wrote the verses that appear in the Bible. Knowing that fear unconsciously treats spiritual concepts as threats, by virtue of the fact human beings wrote down these verses, the concepts they conveyed through the Bible were unavoidably tainted by the fear that allowed those humans to exist. Without question, the Bible is an excellent place to start a spiritual journey, but as long as doctrines govern spiritual quests, their tainted concepts impose constraints on how much growth can occur.

Without Blinders

Once we become adults, we no longer need the level of protection fear afforded us as children, much less want it. This is particularly apparent when we understand how it prevents us from maturing emotionally and, therefore, spiritually. On the surface, emotional growth and spiritual growth might seem mutually exclusive. However, the type of spiritual growth I am proposing is contingent on emotional growth, in particular, a clear understanding of how the lack of emotional growth prevents spiritual growth. Genuine spiritual growth occurs as emotional growth frees the mind from the control of operational fear and the problems it generates.

The good news is that the ability to reach this point is only a choice away. Each time you make that choice, you begin eliminating the film of fear currently covering your perceptions. The ensuing clarity naturally unlocks the recognition of Paradise that Adam and Eve first knew.

Thoughts to Ponder

♦ What religious concepts have you encountered that seem to be contradictions?

♦ What is your experience of unconditional love?

♦ How does the idea that love is a verb affect your perception of love?

Chapter 17

Straddling the Seesaw

magine driving a car with a flat tire. The ride would be choppy—maybe enough to hurt passengers and cause suffering. As discussed earlier, according to the human blueprint, we are spiritual as well as physical beings. Never developing our spiritual sides and living only by the dictates of reality as designated by the physical world is like riding in that car.

Since the days of Adam and Eve, this has been how human beings have functioned. Avatars, prophets, and mystics have tried to show us ways to break free. However, the blindfold that fear unconsciously imposes binds us to this perception of physical reality. We can free ourselves of this blindfold and grow spiritually, but freedom requires *dying to our "selves"*—the beliefs we unconsciously equate with our existence and comprise the identity that other people imposed on us when we were children. This requirement of dying to our "selves" in order to grow spiritually brings to mind Jesus' answer to Nicodemus in John 3:3: "…Except a man be born again he cannot see the kingdom of God."

Born again—when spirit-based love replaced fear as the basis of my belief during my Pivotal Event, that belief that once defined me evaporated. I know I was not the same person as I was before. Was the inexplicable bliss that overcame me at this point a taste of the kingdom of God? That is not for me to say. However, referring to John 3:6, "That which is born of the flesh is flesh; and that which is born of the Spirit is spirit." the fact that bliss, born of the spirit, overcame me the instant love for my aunts replaced the prejudice, would suggest it was.

The Sweet Spot

As pointed out earlier, the crucial point in our creation story occurs when Adam admits he is afraid (Genesis 3:10). This occurs just *after* he and Eve have eaten the forbidden fruit. Even though they have done the unthinkable, at least for a few minutes more, seemingly nothing substantial changes. Adam and Eve *continue interacting with their father* as if it is just another day in Paradise. Despite the fact they are now aware that fear exists, their relationship with God persists as it originated.

It is apparent, from their continuing interactions with their father, that love still prevails. This point is critical. In this regard, it could be said Adam and Eve are straddling the midpoint of a seesaw, teetering between two realities. One end supports their perception of God's love and Paradise. The opposite end supports awareness of fear. Regarding their spiritual and emotional life, at this juncture, they are standing in what I call their *Sweet Spot,* a point of balance between these diametrically opposed realities.

Then their father pops *the* question: did you do it? Of course, God knows they ate the forbidden fruit, if for no other reason than he is omniscient! Knowing this, I had to wonder why God asks this question. If Adam and Eve had confessed, God would have forgiven them and that would have been the end of the story *if* the purpose of the story was to exemplify God's unconditional love.

But the story is not about God's love. Knowing Adam and Eve's reliance on blame exposes the fact their awareness of fear has become operational suggests the story is about what enabled beings of spirit to metamorphose into functioning human beings. Had God not questioned them, they would have remained as originally created with the breath of God—spiritual beings.

The instant answer God by engaging in the "blame game," their seesaw crashes on the side of fear where Adam and Eve encounter emotions for the first time. They were beguiled, alright. Like a neon sign of a pulsating, gyrating Elvis crooning out his songs, emotions that fear began generating were such a novelty, they were as intoxicating as methamphetamines. One encounter and these two innocents were hooked. Their choice to blame switches the nature of fear from being a simple awareness as it originated, to its unconscious, operational aspect. Immediately, fear begins affecting their perceptions.

Once they unknowingly choose fear over trust in their father, as an operational factor, fear begins controlling their minds. Suddenly, everything about their life seems to have changed. They now believe they are separated from God as well as their former home. In light of their altered state, God changes character. The fact is, nothing about God or their former lives actually changed. It's only their perceptions of their lives and the world around them that has changed.

They, as well as we, are still living in the Garden of Eden—our exquisite, blue-green planet. Because Adam and Eve are, and always will be, beings of spirit, it is impossible for them, or for that matter, any human being, to ever be separated from God. However, because they now believe they are separated, the idea of separation, or duality as it is currently understood, replaces their former perception of unity with God.

For Adam and Eve to have the ability to function as human beings, a metamorphosis of this magnitude was precisely what had to happen. Once fear turns operational, returning to the pre-deed Paradise they first knew is neither necessary nor desirable. For that to happen, Adam and Eve would have had to shed their physical bodies—in other words, actually die. On the other hand, they, as well as we, can return to what I call their Sweet Spot—that brief moment in Paradise where these two spirits were straddling the midpoint of their seesaw when awareness of unity with God and awareness of fear were in perfect balance.

Developing the ability to return to this perception of Paradise is the ultimate goal of the spiritual growth I am proposing. All it takes is eliminating the operational aspect of fear by engaging in the emotional growth that the exercises in Chapter 11 address. Once fear no longer controls your thoughts and your behaviors, you can access spiritual truths beyond what the brain is currently capable of comprehending.

Some people might refer to the state of mind of the Sweet Spot as that of a mystic. Could achieving the Sweet Spot be Nirvana? According to sources, Nirvana is transcendence—a matter of living beyond the physical needs and limits of ordinary human experience—removed from the material world. Reaching this state of mind necessitates a form of death—as in dying to ourselves. In this context, dying to ourselves means we have transcended numerous attachments to the physical world; we are no longer the emotional robot that drives ordinary human experience.

However, because we still have a human body and must continue living in this fear-based reality, there will always be problems that cannot be avoided. Emotions will always be able to clog our thoughts and cause conflict. Even though conflicts continue to occur, we now have the tools to resolve them. The world will never be perfect and neither will human beings. However, when our spiritual bodies are as developed as our physical bodies are, we reach our potential as human beings. In my opinion, that is as close to living in Nirvana as I can imagine.

Psychological Death

Dying to ourselves is a psychological form of death that occurs when our dysfunctional childhood beliefs disintegrate. Each psychological death bolsters the mental bridge connecting awareness to our Sweet Spot. This gives us the flexibility to adapt our thoughts according to circumstances as opposed to following the dictates of our programming. Psychological death frees us to observe life more from an eagle's point of view as opposed to that of an ant as distinguished by the lack of emotional growth.

From Ant to Eagle

An eagle's perspective allows a more comprehensive observation of an issue—how even odd aspects of a situation that you might typically discount are, in truth, a necessary element in the makeup of the whole picture. This prospect allows you to make more balanced choices. There is no need to panic, the wolf is just hungry.

Facing a challenging jigsaw puzzle as an ant, armed only with programmed beliefs, would likely cause the ant to retract its antennae and run away—behaving much like an acquaintance of mine did after a recent presidential election. The woman was so overcome with fear she took to her bed for a month. Had she developed an eagle's point of view, this disruption to her life could have been avoided.

Even though an eagle's viewpoint allows us to accept peculiar aspects that we might reject otherwise, does it mean the eagle is inured to the horrors it sees? Of course, it doesn't. The eagle's perspective does prevent the holder from becoming so distraught over disturbing things he observes that he cannot function. During these times of crumbling institutions, this perspective seems especially important.

Maturation

People tend to put spiritual issues on the back burner, promising themselves they'll look at them once life slows down. Nevertheless, the unconscious fear that fuels the physical world, by its very nature, keeps conflict alive. Fear feeds fear. The issues that cause discord and war may quiet down for a while, but that is not peace. The underlying issues will resurface, often in a different costume. The reality that fear feeding fear generates continues to prevail since its emotions first seduced Adam and Eve. If this is still your reality, as the popular saying goes, "How's that working for you?" These days, separation looms, feeding intolerance and fear. Pandemics, climatic changes, war, job loss, migrants moving in stirring up your known world. Chaos is rampant. There's nothing you can control. The old reality is crumbling. Everyone is grieving. Regardless of what you do, every time you look, another wolf is at your door.

The eagle's perspective that comes with spiritual growth frees the mind of judgments that provoke conflict. For an entire day recently, I was bombarded with fear-based thoughts about everything involved in caring for Ken. One side of me wanted to say what was truly on my mind: how much I resented cleaning up after him, his insistence on staying in his chair, never exercising, and most of all, the grief over the loss of the guy who, forty-nine years ago, sent me a get-well card when strep throat forced me to cancel our first date. Without my spiritual side interceding, expressing these unfettered thoughts could have so enraged him it would have taken hours to calm him down. The fact that I was straddling my Sweet Spot during this period allowed me to embrace the bigger picture of our years together before dementia set in, which saved the day.

It seems presumptuous, heretical to even hint, due to its religious implications, that I have been born of the spirit. Only because it goes against traditional interpretations that human minds have attached to Christ's words could it be called heretical. The first time I *consciously* connected with my spirit during my Pivotal Event could be thought of being born of the (my) spirit.

The spiritual growth I am proposing in which love replaces fear as the basis of our thoughts opens the mind to the awareness of our spirit. The first experience we have that consciously brings us face to face with our spirits is transformative. As happened to me, I was not the same person as I was before. I truly felt I had been born of my spirit.

By reaching the point where I was straddling my seesaw, the perspective that resulted resolved the conundrum the five words from my dream posed that— love is all that exists.

Thoughts to Ponder

♦ Think about the current news reports in terms of fight-or-flight situations. Now try to imagine the outcome of each situation if those in charge were straddling their Sweet Spots.

♦ Imagine how different your life would be if the basis of most of your thoughts was love.

Chapter 18

Love *Is* All That Exists

O*nly* after fear turned operational and altered their perceptions did Adam and Eve come to believe they no longer were living in the Garden of Eden. The pictures of Earth that astronauts have sent back convince me that Adam and Eve never left Paradise. Fear had simply begun controlling the way they thought.

Our exquisite blue-green Earth *is* the Garden of Eden. Paradise, or the Garden of Eden, is merely a love-based perception of the world, the result of spiritual growth. Once Adam and Eve became capable of functioning as human beings, they lacked the capacity to comprehend the truth of their reality.

Questionable Security

One simple, but significant, misconception we unconsciously hold allows our outgrown childhood beliefs to continue manifesting wolves (conflicts)—the security our brains unconsciously equate with these beliefs. In reality, this form of security vanishes with death; therefore, it is only an *illusion* of security. The only real security that these beliefs promise is that the Paleolithic emotions they generate will never stop fueling the medieval behaviors indicative of the human condition. Even when cloaked in metaphorical sheepskins and seemingly harmless, they are not. The impact of my Granddaddy's belief in the sin of eating meat on Friday, my church's refusal to honor the environment— the list of the problems they create is endless.

Each human being fabricates wolves unique to the story of their lives. These varmints indeed blow down houses, destroy peoples' lives, and will keep fomenting atrocities, such as war, until we realize their source lies in our childish mindsets and stop blaming or justifying bad behavior. As an emotionally mature adult, we can take responsibility for our detrimental actions. The ability to admit we were in the wrong can bring an end to tragedies of this nature. All that is required is to engage in emotional and, therefore, spiritual growth.

In spirit's reality, all that exists is love. Peace is its distinguishing characteristic.

Psychological Death

As has been pointed out, our current perception of reality relies on our beliefs rooted in fear. Together with its promise of security, it is an illusion. The only true form of security available to us lies with the spirit each of us carries into this life at birth. Psychological death shifts the epicenter of our human definition of security, currently based on fear, back to awareness of our innate spirit.

As unconditional love replaces fear, I benefit, and everyone with whom I come into contact does as well. Because I've accepted my greedy side, I no longer judge people when I see them expressing greed. Instead of rejecting them as I once did, I feel compassion for them. Much of what I see, say, and do is and will always be fear-based, because I am a human being. However, my thoughts and actions increasingly lack judgement and express love.

Once fear no longer restricts choices, a true paradigm shift occurs. The immutability of the human condition dissipates. Suffering and war are no longer forgone conclusions. Without beliefs preordaining our actions, constructive, win-win outcomes become possible. The choices before us become unlimited. Without the emotional interference from fear, we can adapt according to circumstances, which in light of the increasing chaos worldwide, will help us surf the problems that come our way.

Because I am human I am and will always be imperfect. I will continue making mistakes, they are how I learn. Life will always be a challenge; it is just part of being born into this fear-based reality. As long as I have a body most of what I believe will remain rooted in fear. In spite of this, the awareness that results from spiritual growth allows me to become the sovereign of my life, not the victim.

Who Woulda Thunk?

I suspect the authors of Vatican II could never have imagined that their decrees would inadvertently lead to someone questioning all beliefs as well as a reconfigured interpretation of the verses in Genesis 3, which has been crucial to the concept of sin. A psychological analysis of these verses offers a more positive interpretation. This analysis cancels out the traditional idea of Adam and Eve's "fall" by unveiling the critical role Adam's discovery of fear played in allowing beings of spirit to function as human beings. It has also exposed beliefs as illusions—beliefs we are so attached to that they control our lives—childhood beliefs that can affect the rest of a person's life, and along the way affect their children's lives, too.

For example, Mother's definitive incident happened when she was five. Having just recovered from a bout of measles, she wanted to visit her best friend, Honey.

Having gotten permission from her mother, Babo, to leave the house, Mother was walking down the front walk when her inebriated father caught sight her and became enraged. He ran after her and asked where she thought she was going. Mother told him, adding Babo had given her permission to go. Perhaps it was because Mother hadn't asked for *his* permission, who knows? Immediately, he picked her up, put her under his arm, and marched back into the house. He then stuffed her into a small closet under their staircase and locked the door. Mother told me she was so angry she pledged there and then never to let anyone "get" to her again and make her cry. And she didn't. It became the source of her cold indifference to me, and most everyone else too. This incident revealed the source of Mother's Teflon heart and its impacts that never stopped surprising me.

Long after Agnes died, I visited Mother just after she got up from her afternoon nap. Bypassing the usual chitchat, Mother launched into recalling the dream she had just had that haunted her. In this dream, unexpectedly, Agnes was packing up, intending to leave Mother's employ. When she approached Mother with news of her imminent departure, Agnes told her she had been so good to her over the years she wanted to give Mother something special to remember her by. At this point Mother said she woke up.

Out of curiosity, I asked her how she felt about the prospect of Agnes suddenly leaving her. Inconvenienced was her answer. Inconvenienced? The raw lack of feeling over losing her loyal employee and confidante of forty-plus years astounded me. At the same time, it was most revealing. I suspect the belief her five-year-old brain had conceived precipitated Mother's indifference, not just in this dream to Agnes, but to me and to everyone who knew her.

Resolution

Curiosity about Mother's cold heart initiated the quest that has given rise to this book.

As destructive as childhood beliefs can be, they serve as trellises that support the growth that makes us unique human beings. Once we no longer need their support, they begin falling apart, and when they do, they generate conflict. Our inability to recognize when our beliefs have become dysfunctional together with our lack of knowledge about how to eliminate the problems they cause work to keep us subservient to the human condition.

Vatican II inadvertently has given us the gift of choice, the choice to control our lives or remain vassals of our fears. Choice gives us the ability to switch from a fear-based perception of life to a love-based perception. By making the choice to switch we can return to that point in Paradise when Adam and Eve were straddling their Sweet Spot. As happened with Adam and Eve at this crucial point, we too will have the awareness to interact with spirit as well as the ability perceive Paradise.

The elimination of the unconscious, operational element of fear makes it clear—all that exists really is love.

The completion of Exercise #1: Good Parenting offers us the ability to create a more peaceful existence by eliminating the dysfunctional beliefs that foment conflict.

The essence of God is *what we are;* human beings are *who we are.* Unconscious fear, the sole factor that creates the perception of who we are, allows us, as God's progeny, to function as human beings. Thus, unconscious fear that allows us to function as human beings, by any label placed on its effects, be it sin, mistake, or flaw, was the perfect imperfection.

Acknowledgements

I am especially grateful to those brave souls who worked with me as I refined my theories during their rough beginnings. I owe a special thanks to my husband, Ken, who gave me the freedom to pursue my endeavors.

I want to thank Kate Victory Hannisian, the one editor who patiently helped me plow through the initial version of this book. I also want to thank Stuart Waldner, whose editing helped me unravel and clarify many ideas I found difficult to articulate.

Special thanks to my friends at Earthlight for allowing me to draw upon parts of Samuel's exercises.

About the Author

Catherine Tuggle didn't set out to be a writer. She was a successful, professional visual artist for twelve years before the profound events she began experiencing compelled her to begin writing.

Perpetually creative, Catherine continues to explore writing poetry, sketching, painting, knitting, sewing, cooking, reading, drywall masonry, playing the piano, gardening, and designing whatever catches her interest. She is an avid dog lover. Her most recent canine side-kick is a German shepherd named Reacher.

Resumé

ACADEMIC CREDENTIALS
B.A. Lawrence University, 1966

CONTINUING EDUCATION
Numerous Watercolor Workshops through 1978
One year painting at Louisville School of Art 1978
Two years drawing at University of Louisville 1980, 1981
One semester painting at University of Louisville 1990

EXHIBITIONS AND SHOWS

1977   *"Woman's Show,"* University of Kentucky, Lexington, KY

1981   *"8 State Exhibition in Graphics,"* J. B. Speed Art Museum, Louisville, KY

1981   *"Earth I,"* Art Center Association, Louisville, KY

1983   One Woman Show, Yvonne Rapp Gallery, Louisville, KY

1983   *"Realism Today,"* Evansville Museum of Arts and Sciences, Evansville, IN

1984   One Woman Show, Yvonne Rapp Gallery, Louisville, KY

1986   *"Lines of Communication."* Group Show, sponsored by Art Center Association, Louisville, KY

1986   One Woman Show, Yvonne Rapp Gallery, Louisville, KY

1987   *"In Celebration,"* One Woman Show, Yvonne Rapp Gallery, Louisville, KY

1987   *"Pastel Anthology II,"* Group Show, Grace Borgenicht Gallery, New York, NY

1988   *"To Life,"* One Woman Show, Yvonne Rapp Gallery, Louisville, KY

1988   *"Me,"* Group Self-Portrait Show, Liberty Gallery, Louisville, KY

1989   *"In Sight of Louisville: A Perspective of Louisville Artists,"* Group Show, The Washington Design Center, Washington, D.C.

1990   Annual Show, Yvonne Rapp Gallery, Louisville, KY

1992   One Woman Show, Yvonne Rapp Gallery, Louisville, KY

CORPORATE COLLECTIONS
Beaver Dam Bank, Beaver Dam, KY
Citizens Fidelity Bank & Trust Company, Louisville, KY
J.J. Hilliard - W.L. Lyons, Inc., Louisville, KY
Kentucky Fried Chicken Corporation, Louisville, KY

Notes

1. Chinese Proverb: *Chinese Proverbs from Olden Times* (Mount Vernon, New York: Peter Pauper Press, 1956).

2. Bible, King James Version (Cleveland and New York: The World Publishing Company, 1945).

3. The Second Ecumenical Council of the Vatican, commonly known as the Second Vatican Council or Vatican II, addressed relations between the Catholic Church and the modern world from October 1962 to December 8, 1965.

4. Jewish Virtual Library, https://www.jewishvirtuallibrary.org/.

5. Father Greg Boyle, *Tattoos on the Heart: The Power of Boundless Compassion* (Free Press, 2011).

6. Emotions: Webster's Ninth New Collegiate Dictionary.

7. Flannery O'Connor, *The Complete Stories* (Farrar, Straus and Giroux, 1982).

8. National Public Radio Study, "High Incomes Don't Bring You Happiness," September 7, 2010, https://www.npr.org>sections>money>2010/09/07.

9. Harry M. Caudill, *Night Comes to the Cumberlands: A biography of a Depressed Area,* page 50. (An *Atlantic Monthly Press Book,* Little, Brown and Company, Boston-Toronto, 1963.

10. Colin Blakemore and Grahame F. Cooper. "Development of the Brain Depends on the Visual Environment," *Nature,* 228, 477-478 (1970). https://www.nature.com/articles/228477a0.

11. Quotes from Thomas Merton, *Conjectures of a Guilty Bystander*, as featured on Goodreads, https://www.goodreads.com/work/quotes/404737.

12. The Book of Common Prayer, 1944, Thomas Nelson and Sons, New York, page 82.